GETTING OUT FROM UNDER

How To Break Free From Stress And Overwhelm To Get The Life You Have Always Wanted

JEANNETTE HAY

The Overwhelm Coach
Award Winning Author

Limits of Liability and Disclaimer of Warranty

The author and publisher shall not be liable for your misuse of this material. This book is strictly for informational and educational purposes.

Warning – Disclaimer

The purpose of this book is to educate and entertain. The author and/or publisher do not guarantee that anyone following these techniques, suggestions, tips, ideas, or strategies will become successful.

The author and/or publisher shall have neither liability nor responsibility to anyone with respect to any loss or damage caused, or alleged to be caused, directly or indirectly, by the information contained in this book.

Copyright © 2020 Jeannette Hay

All rights reserved.

www.GettingOutFromUnderBook.com

No part of this publication may be reproduced, distributed, or transmitted in any form or by any means, including photocopying, recording, or other electronic or mechanical methods, without the prior written permission of the publisher, except in the case of brief quotations embodied in reviews and certain other non-commercial uses permitted by copyright law.

ISBN: 978-1-77277-347-7

DEDICATION

I would like to dedicate this book to all my previous clients who were brave enough to open up their hearts and minds and show me their fears and desires. You taught me so much while accompanying you on your journey in creating a happier life for yourself and for those around you, and I am grateful for the experience.

To my best friend, Sean, words cannot express my appreciation for having you in my life all these years. Thank you for being you and for just being here.

TABLE OF CONTENTS

Foreword vii
Acknowledgements ix
Introduction... 1
Chapter 1: The Dreaded Dwindling Spiral 11
Chapter 2: The Hidden Power Of Predictability... 21
Chapter 3: The Power Of Simplicity...................... 31
Chapter 4: What Has Clutter Got To Do With It?... 45
Chapter 5: The Growing Epidemic........................ 61
Chapter 6: The Deadliest Of Diseases.................. 73
Chapter 7: Yes, Your Health Is At Risk 83
Chapter 8: Shame, Blame, And Regrets............... 91
Chapter 9: Breaking Through To Your Own Success! 99
Chapter 10: Bringing 4 Simple Words Into
Your Professional Life 105
About The Author.. 115
Testimonials.. 117
Note From The Author 125

FOREWORD

Are you dealing with different levels of stress, which have left you feeling overwhelmed and exhausted? Author Jeannette Hay understands those feelings all too well, and in *Getting Out From Under: How To Break Free From Stress And Overwhelm To Get The Life You Have Always Wanted*, she lays out the tools you need to successfully reduce and manage your stress.

After sharing various experiences highlighting how overwhelming and stressful life can become, Jeannette focuses on how you can reduce stress, starting with using her *4 Simple Words and Golden Timer* techniques. Once you have these techniques and put them into practice, you will see immediate relief. She gives you the skills and knowledge to recognize the source of your stress and start the process of destressing your life, so that you can live the life you have always dreamed of.

Every part of her guide contains nuggets that you can easily implement into your daily life. These small changes can lead to significant results, ones that can positively impact your relationships, both personally and professionally. No matter where your stress is coming from, Jeannette can help you to get organized and take control over the aspects of your life that leave you feeling overwhelmed and stressed out.

Give yourself the gift of stress reduction and pick up this amazing guide that taps into the power of *4 Simple Words*!

Raymond Aaron
New York Times Bestselling Author

ACKNOWLEDGEMENTS

My parents, Penney and Tony Hay, taught me to love the unknown and revel in its unveiling. I have my mother to thank for teaching me to love and appreciate the small moments in life that cost nothing but filled my soul with joy.

Sean Ford, my rock, my supporter, confidant and dearest friend and companion, who has been there for me in so many ways over the years, it would take a book to list them all. Sometimes you know me better than I know myself! I know you have my back, and I will always have yours.

Julian Hay, my brother, who has come to my aide whenever I have needed him. We have gone through a lot together over the years and have a special bond that will never break.

Janet Wilcox, my great friend and fellow author and mentor. We started out as client and professional organizer, and over the years have experienced many things together and created a wonderful friendship that has helped each of us grow and solve problems. Thank you for your encouragement and for having such a kind and generous heart.

Harold Taylor, a generous person and time management genius, whose wisdom I have happily absorbed over the years. You have helped me sort out things in my head when I was questioning what to do. You are a stabilizing part of my life.

Helen Goodman, my longest friendship that I have, and one that continues to enrich my life, just by you being your indomitable, generous-hearted self. I do not have to explain myself to you, because you have known me for so long. Love that aspect of our relationship!

Naveed Hyder, what can I say to my dearest friend and artistic, creative thinking friend? We two have laughed so hard that we cried and have supported each other through the years in numerous ways. You always show me you want the best for me, and I hope you know I wish the same for you. Thank you for continuing to be in my life.

Betty Hynes, my soul-sister, no matter how long we have been apart, once we get together, it is as though we spoke the day before. We just naturally pick up where we left off. I understand how rare this is, and I value your friendship dearly. You are my sister from another mother! I feel my most authentic with you, and effortlessly can share my deepest concerns with you, knowing that you can handle them and give me good advice, which I may not want to hear but need to hear.

Andy Hoare, my friend, mentor, and so much more. Thanks to you, I am more able and capable, with increased clarity of thought, and you showed me that something can always be done about it!

Marilyn Anthony, my mentor in professional organizing, and always my advisor and dear friend. We have weathered countless situations and always prevailed; together we are unstoppable. Your confidence in my abilities has empowered me to never give up.

Lisa Bell, who always brings aesthetics into my life and never fails to help me relax and enjoy life more. We have worked so well together in various scenarios and have grown so much through them. You are a terrific friend and a great listener!

Bobbi Benson, friend, client, and ex-mother-in-law; a combo that has endured, and I am the richer for it. Thank you for continuing to include me in your life so that we can have more laughs, good food, and fun experiences together. You are special.

George Alger, a dear friend and ally, who has taught me by showing me what can be accomplished with tenacity along a given line towards a goal, and who reminds me of the need in me to also function within the art world, always creating. Thank you for continuing to be in my life.

Mary Ford, so many great giggles together, as well as deep philosophical discussions that I enjoy so much. As an ex-mother-in-law and friend, I love that we have so much in common (aside from your son) and appreciate the finer things in life, like flowers and food! Thank you for always being so authentic and direct.

Kleo Tobias, my dear, fun, creative, open-hearted, and generous friend. You always get me laughing, and I admire your constant creative quilting and fiber art abilities so much. My fellow artist and appreciator of wonderful colour combos, Dim Sum, and new experiences, I am richer from having you in my life!

Dr. Mandana Attarzadeh, recipient of the 2020 "Woman of Worth Award" from International Women Achievers Award, you deserve all things good coming to you. I'm so happy that we met all those years ago; it was meant to be!

Anita Colussi-Zanon, fellow author and artist; more than a client, you have become a valued friend.

Marlene Marco, founder of The Heart of Networking, who has always been ready to listen and give sane advice to me. Thank you for being there for me on many occasions.

Susan Gould, for always being so supportive and such a cheerleader of my abilities. You never fail to make me feel good and validated.

Miss Wallace, my first English teacher, who lit a flame in me for writing and reading.

The Girl Guides of Devonshire in England, I will always be grateful to them for teaching me the importance in being prepared and resilient.

Dr. Jason Fung, I am forever grateful for his wisdom and example of personal courage, and for breaking out of one's comfort zone for the betterment of others. You are a lifesaver.

L. Ron Hubbard, whose wisdom and example of helping others has always been inspirational in my life.

INTRODUCTION

Our world is changing rapidly. It has become one of fast-paced soundbites and constant information overload. It can be difficult to navigate this changing world successfully, and for this reason I have provided you with solutions for how to navigate it with less stress and feelings of being overwhelmed.

In today's fast-paced society, with constant demands for our attention and decisions, more people are experiencing anxiety, fatigue, stress, overwhelm, and increased dissatisfaction in their work and life balance. Add to that the feeling of having too much to do and not enough time to do it all, and you have a recipe for disaster. Consequently, people are trying to do too much all at once in an attempt to save time. It might appear that multi-tasking works, but the result is lowered productivity and an ever-increasing level of frustration and stress.

Something can be done about it. You don't have to live with this constant state of running without getting anywhere. I will explain the tools you need for you to be able to recognise where your stress is coming from, and how to start the process of destressing your life.

Solving Your Problem of Not Enough Time (or How to Expand Time)

I felt compelled to write *Getting Out From Under,* so that you can find out why you feel as if you cannot get ahead and never have enough time to get things done, or know what you can do to stop feeling like that. When you are struggling with physical and mental clutter, this book will show you how to actively unclutter your mind and environment. At the same time, you will start to feel empowered as you increase your focus, gain clarity, and ultimately be successful with your life.

If you are an executive seeking to accelerate your career with an improved work/life balance and want to make better decisions and move beyond your challenges, then this book is for you. I have written this for when you are struggling with procrastination and feelings of being overwhelmed, or for when you just want to reduce your stress level without sacrificing your level of productivity. The advice in this small, easy-to-follow, how-to guidebook is designed to empower you to take back control of your life and live beyond your fears into the life you have always dreamed of having.

For more than fifteen years, I have been a professional organizer as a member of the Professional Organizers in Canada, which is the national association that represents professional organizers across Canada. Within this association, I currently hold the highest membership level, that of Gold Leaf. In the past, I have served as an Executive Board member, Vice Chair, and Chair to the Toronto Chapter of Professional

Organizers in Canada, while uncluttering and organizing hundreds of clients' minds and spaces. As *The Overwhelm Coach,* I have helped hundreds of clients create *Clarity, Focus, and Success,* while reducing their feelings of overwhelm in their lives.

Teachers, students, business executives, housewives, entrepreneurs, and CEOs have all experienced success using these techniques. This book concentrates on the two most basic steps, ones that will immediately reduce your stress level. This first step is called *4 Simple Words,* and the second is *The Golden Timer.* When you learn to apply them, your life will change forever.

One of my clients, Fred, worked with me to declutter his life. I started him out with the first step, *4 Simple Words,* which gave him a sense of empowerment. "For the first time in my professional life, I feel in control of my time. My energy level has actually gone up, because I don't feel exhausted by a never-ending to-do list. I love Jeannette!"

You have read this far in the book because you know your procrastination and lack of knowledge in time management is drowning you. So why not be that "take action" person that you have always wanted to be? Continue reading and start applying the tools and skills in this book right now, and you will be. What have you got to lose except your stress, anxiety, and feelings of overwhelm?

The productivity and organizational time management tools, and dependable time-tested systems, in my book, will create a solid foundation for you to create positive successful habits to be your foundation throughout your life's journey.

Your growing sense of empowerment will enable you to have more time for the things that are essential to your values, beliefs, and purpose.

You will gain the ability to focus on what is important to you, while lessening your stress, thus giving you a higher level of clarity and more of a winning mindset. And it is easy to get this, as all you have to do is keep reading!

My Story as to How I Got Here

For years I would help friends and family with their paperwork, uncluttering and organizing their spaces. They hated doing it, and I loved to do it. Simple. Everybody won! It made me a great personal assistant, but I also started to notice common themes when we dug into the underlying "why" the clutter existed.

People were always saying to me, "Oh, you should be an organizer." I thought they were just making a joke. I had no idea that such a profession actually existed. Honestly, I thought that people had to do this for themselves or find a friend/employee who could step in and unclutter for them. I had no idea that there was a whole profession wrapped around the idea of uncluttering, organizing, and increased productivity.

Then one day, after helping my (last) boss's wife unclutter and organize her children's playroom, she echoed the same thing about how I should become a professional organizer. As usual, I was ready to brush the topic off, but then she showed me a magazine article on the joys of organizing, written by a professional organizer. I was intrigued. That same night, I found the website for the Professional Organizers in Canada, and immediately signed up. By the next week, I was working for myself in my new company called, *Get Me Organized!* My experience helping others allowed me to open a business and stay focused during the process of building my clientele.

I have held many different jobs in my life, and I have moved numerous times and lived in multiple countries. Not only did I have to stay organized, because of moving that much, but I also recognized the cultural impact as I soaked in life outside of my home country. Consequently, I can relate to just about any life challenges faced by my clients. I too have experienced the emotional decision-making process of what to get rid of and what to keep as I packed for yet another move. I too have yearned for more time to do the things I really love to do, and desired to spend less time on the duties that I had to get done.

I came to understand that the problem for many of us is that we don't have the right tools to stay above water in this busy life we lead. The result is that I was like you, living in a comfort zone that wasn't really that comfortable, but it was what I knew.

Consequently, I became one of my own clients, putting my steps into practice on a personal level. The results have been amazing and made me even more determined to share my knowledge with you.

Because I have been a speaker, workshop host and executive, president, chair, board member, entrepreneur, grass roots community-based founder, and "animal fine artist" for many years, I have yet to come across a situation that my clients are struggling with that I have not experienced myself. So, I have the empathy for what they are going through and can gently guide them to a successful resolution.

Your life doesn't have to be a constant stream of feeling overwhelmed and stressed, with never enough time because of the demands on your time.

I am going to help you stretch outside your comfort zone mentally and learn for yourself what has brought you to this less than happy place in your life, and how you can change things for the better. Something can be done about it.

> *"If I have the belief that I can do it, I will surely acquire the capacity to do it, even if I may not have it at the beginning."*
>
> **Mahatma Gandhi**, Indian Lawyer, Politician, Writer

When coaching my clients, I tell them that mental as well as physical clutter, often created by procrastination, are some of the issues they have to deal with in moving forward.

But growth and success are born out of failures, so just keep going!

There is one thing that I can't do for you, and that is provide the motivation to change. I can't identify your "why." You have to find the motivation within yourself for a better life.

But I can still be of help to you—so ask yourself:

- Am I sick and tired of running from one activity to the next, with no breaks?
- Am I missing out on time with loved ones, because I have too many things to juggle?
- Has my clutter complicated my life, making it difficult to find important documents or notes?
- Do I find myself constantly running behind, from appointment to appointment?
- When I arrive at appointments or meetings, is my professional reputation compromised because I am ill-prepared or disorganized?
- Am I always spending precious time looking for everyday items?
- Am I being financially impacted by late bills, simply because I can't find them?
- Am I just plain tired of being stressed out?
- Is my home more stressful than it is relaxing?

All these questions can help you to identify your "why," the seat of your motivation. After all, there are going to be parts of this journey that are challenging as you step outside of your comfort zone. Understanding why you are doing it in the first place will help you to keep going during those challenging moments.

Your motivation is key here. Throughout this book, I will show you what ordinary people, just like you, have to say about how their life has been changed for the better through the application of these easy steps. They took the plunge and went outside their comfort zone, and just as I promised, their life improved. My hope is that their testimonials will provide additional motivation for you to step beyond your zone of comfort into a new world of possibilities, leaving behind the limitations of your clutter, overwhelm, and disorganization.

This is a "**Motivational Moment**":

At the time I met her, Enza was a busy entrepreneur, running a very successful interior design business, as well as being a wife and mother to two busy teenagers. She would have a pad of paper next to her bed so that when she woke in the night, she could write down her ideas or things she thought she might forget. In short, she was on a non-stop cycle. There was no time to pause, reflect, or relax. That ultimately impacted her family, business, and personal relationships. Not to mention, it was exhausting for her.

Then we met, and she grabbed the tools I gave her; and she has not looked back since. This is what she has to say:

"My time with Jeannette was invaluable... when you are running a small business, you have little time to organize, so getting Jeannette to help me was the best decision for getting it done! I use all the things she

taught me, each and every day, and I have more room in my head for creative thoughts and planning now that Jeannette 'GOT ME ORGANIZED.'

Thanks, Jeannette, for everything . . . especially my new color-coded filing—it is soooo beautiful!"

Enza Tiberi-Checchia, Mental Health Advocate; Speaker & Founder, mietcetera.com; Chief Visionary Officer & Co-Founder, hatsonforawareness.com

Chapter 1

THE DREADED DWINDLING SPIRAL

Usually, when you feel that you are losing control of your life, you patch together a system for yourself that sort of, kind of, works for a while. Then as things get easier, you drop that system, figuring that you can handle it all now. Gradually, things start to build back up again, and you find yourself feeling overpowered and overwhelmed yet again. So, what do you do? Exhausted, overwhelmed, and stressed, you pull out your old "system" and put it back into play again. Most people do this repeatedly throughout their life; it is a never-ending cycle of hope and loss. That system becomes the Band-Aid of your life, without addressing any of the underlying reasons why you became overwhelmed in the first place. Consequently, you never address those causes, and the Band-Aid keeps falling off, and you keep putting it back on.

> *"The definition of insanity is doing the same thing over and over again, expecting a different result."*
>
> **Albert Einstein**, German-born theoretical physicist who developed the theory of relativity

I think you will agree it is time for a different strategy. You need a system that actually works every time you need it to successfully put you back into control of your life. It needs to be one that isn't just an ineffective Band-Aid, but a true solution to the clutter, stress, and disorganization that has claimed your life.

So just pull off your Band-Aid, and dump it in the trash.

The Dirty Little Secret

As *The Overwhelm Coach,* I can say that the majority of my clients come to me feeling trapped, struggling with haunting feelings of failure. They, like you, have battled these thoughts constantly, some for many years, feeling too ashamed to ask for help, and all the while feeling overwhelmed, powerless, stressed, and alone. In the meantime, their "dirty little secret" of failing to manage their life in a better manner, to achieve the dreams they have always had in their head, are continuing to make them feel inadequate, miserable, and unproductive. Their disappointment in themselves results in this dwindling spiral of quiet desperation, frustration, and mounting stress levels, resulting in a foggy thought process based in confusion.

It just keeps compounding, as these feelings feed even more negative thoughts. Your reality is impacted by your thoughts, and the process just keeps reinforcing the tendency to clutter, creating even more clutter and disorganization in your life. You start to feel that you are never going to get out of this endless loop. Often, you keep reaching out for the next latest and greatest app, or read the newest blog, hoping that it will contain the magical answer you need so that you can fix all your issues.

Sound familiar?

If you see yourself reflected in what I have written, then you need to know that you are not alone at all; in fact, the majority of people I have met, secretly feel trapped in exactly the same way. Over the years, I have observed that everyone, just like you, is overwhelmed to some degree in their life. For some, it is just one small area of their life that is out of control, and for others, they feel completely overwhelmed by their entire life.

> *"Always be a first-rate version of yourself instead of a second-rate version of somebody else."*
>
> **Judy Garland**, American singer and actress

Some statistics from the POC (Professional Organizers in Canada Association) state that actually 8 out of 10 Canadians feel overwhelmed. They feel there is not enough time to get everything done. They have too much "stuff" to deal with. More people than you can imagine are feeling the exact same way that you are feeling right now, across the world.

If you have feelings of overwhelm, and you know that you (obviously) lack the skills to deal with it, then the answers are here for you within this book.

Imagine how the next generation feels. They have been watching us struggle with not enough time and mounting stress and have started thinking that living this lifestyle is normal.

According to a 2018 Statistics Canada report, the younger generation are feeling more stressed than in the past. Canadians who are 15 years of age or older have reported that they felt "quite a bit" or "extremely stressful" most days, and that number rises to 30 per cent, specifically among the 35 to 54 age group. With that level of constant stress, no wonder anxiety and depression numbers continue to rise. Having the right tools to counteract this can be critical to modeling a different way of living, one that is less stressful and uncluttered.

There was a survey done a couple of years ago on stress levels of different generations. It was determined that while Millennials (ages 18 to 33) and Gen Xers (ages 34 to 47) report the highest average stress levels, Boomers (ages 48 to 66) and Matures (ages 67 and older) join them in reporting levels that are higher than they consider healthy. Add to that the latest reports that adolescents are reporting feeling stressed and are having an increase in panic attacks and suicides, and you have a good reason to live a much-simplified life.

Keeping It All Together (On the Outside)

To outsiders, your life may look successful, but on the inside, you may be concealing the fact that you are feeling overwhelmed, exhausted, and inadequate. The harder you try to keep it all together, the more burned out you feel. Your various attempts to keep this façade up are failing, and you start to feel it all crumble under you.

I have found that whether I am speaking on stage to an audience, or running a workshop, it is the same for each of you. Even though you want to, you cannot reach out for help from people you know, simply because you have done such a good job on selling yourself as successful, and you don't feel that you can pull back the curtain now and bare your soul. Sound familiar?

Everyone has a limit on the amount of stress that they can live with while still making sane decisions and being productive. You may feel that you are permanently trapped within your procrastination and feelings of being powerless to change things, but you can actually break free of it all. You can really turn things around so that you can live a life where you can have clarity and focus, with increased production, and all of it with less stress. Becoming a workaholic, which involves working longer and longer hours, does not guarantee success. In fact, it has been proven to lessen your ability to succeed in life. So that is not the sustainable solution you were hoping for.

As an example of how working long hours are not the guarantee for success, I give you this example from the past.

If you had been working during the Industrial Revolution, a normal day would have consisted of 10 to 16 hours of work, getting a few hours of sleep, and getting back to it the next day. Then one day, Henry Ford (founder of the Ford car company) decided to experiment with a less stressful, eight-hour workday. This was a revolutionary idea at the time. As a result, not only did he find his workers were more productive on an hourly basis, but they were more productive overall.

With their improved work environment being more pleasant, his company's profit margins doubled within two years. Other companies followed his example until we now have the standard of an eight-hour workday. Despite this example of higher productivity from less hours worked, part of our culture has actually started going back in time, toward working those longer days, despite the evidence that it does not contribute to more productivity or happier employees.

This will only lead to more stress and lower quality of life again. Crazy!

On the other hand, you have more progressive companies striking back and questioning if even the eight-hour day is still the most successful model. They are opting for flexible work hours and nap rooms with beds for their employees. They are concentrating more on the levels of production from an employee, versus the number of hours they clock in for work. Thankfully, this is a growing trend. If the goal is to increase productivity, and by the end of the week, the employee produces the same amount of work in a shorter period of time than another worker, and this translates into a happier employee with a more simplified, less stressful life, then why not? We all win.

However, for this to change, you need to do things differently, creating new habits that are made easier to establish if you have someone to help you. If you want more details on how you can be coached by me on getting to this better place in your life, then simply go to: www.GettingOutFromUnderBook.com/Coaching.

There is a lot to be said in creating more simplicity in your life, as well as regularly taking breaks, taking a walk, or napping without feeling guilty. Re-energising your mind and body to feel refreshed and less stressed has been proven to improve mental and physical health, as well as productivity.

Understand that to pull yourself out of this downward spiral, then you will need to face or confront a few things that will take you out of your comfort zone. There is an expression: "The Devil you know versus the Devil you don't." You may want to make changes in your life, but the fear of letting go of the "familiar" can stop you. Your comfort zone is full of stressful and overwhelming aspects, yet you cling to them simply because they are comfortably familiar. Those comfort and familiar moments are becoming an anchor, weighing you down instead of lifting you up.

Like you, most people live within their fears, not their dreams. It takes courage to rise above your fears and break past the borders of your comfort zone. But once you have broken through your self-imposed barriers, the rewards are definitely worth the effort.

> "I learned that courage was not the absence of fear, but the triumph over it. The brave man is not he who does not feel afraid, but he who conquers that fear."
>
> **Nelson Mandela**, South African, served as President of South Africa, anti-apartheid revolutionary, political leader, and philanthropist

Your limiting beliefs in your abilities, eroded over time, is causing you to waste your potential and your entire lifetime in dissatisfaction and, at best, limited success.

When your actions become more stable, the natural result is more simplicity. When your life becomes simpler, then the stress starts to drop away. By learning the power hidden within the application of just *4 Simple Words,* consisting of *predictability, simplicity,* and *stress relief,* you will have tools that will always help you to have a simpler, calmer, more successful life, with a lot less negative drama in it.

4 Simple Words That Can Change Your Life

There are four very simple and yet deceptively powerful words that, when applied to your life, can be the foundation for your success and relief, as they have been for hundreds of my clients over the years. If you are now honestly thinking to yourself, "How can these words change my life?" you will be surprised. Read on . . .

These words have power within their definitions and the concepts that they represent. Using them to create habits and actions within your life will be key to making dramatic changes for you, even before you complete the process of getting out from under overwhelm. Over the next few pages and chapters, I am going to define these words and give you a deeper understanding of their concepts.

I would like to ensure that we both have the exact same definition and understanding of the words I will be using in this how-to guidebook:

Predictability – Anything that you can see or know before it happens is predictable; to make known in advance.

Simple – Meaning easily understood or done, presenting no difficulty.

Simplicity – Comes from the word *simple*, meaning easily understood or done, presenting no difficulty.

Procrastination – The action of delaying or postponing something, or putting off, especially something requiring immediate attention.

Overwhelmed – To overpower the thoughts, emotions, or senses in a very powerful way; a mixture of depression and stress.

If you are ready for more clarity and an improved, productive mindset, then you have come to the right place. The anxiety, fatigue, stress, and feelings of being overwhelmed and powerless to change things for the better, will lessen as you put these four simple words into practice.

Now let's start this journey together, and explore the first of these concepts, namely *predictability*, in the next chapter.

Chapter 2

THE HIDDEN POWER OF PREDICTABILITY

Welcome to stepping out of your comfort zone and into the next process of positive change in your life. I congratulate you for your personal bravery. Anything that you can see or know before it happens is therefore *predictable*—to make something known in advance, giving people information that they can count on. Predictability is something that we long for, because it means that things are stable and constant. There are no sudden unexpected surprises or drama in predictability.

That stability also contributes to your ability to determine with reasonable certainty the impact of your thoughts and actions, which comes straight from your prior predictable actions. It is a well-known fact that positive thoughts often lead to positive actions, whereas negative thoughts often lead to negative actions. So, let's talk about what happens when you have little or no predictability in your life.

When things are not consistent in your life, then you can experience various negative and often dramatic effects. When things are not where they are supposed to be, or when your relationships suffer because you are constantly trying to make amends for missed expectations, or worse yet, you are beating yourself up because you keep missing the mark and disappointing your own personal expectations, this can be overwhelming.

For example, if you come down in the morning, needing to drive off somewhere, and you cannot find your car keys, then this immediately creates unpredictable actions and thoughts in your life. You might start panicking, thinking about traffic, what it means for your ability to actually be on time, or how it will put you behind at work.

The Grumpy Start to Your Day

Whether you are late for work and, of course, whether you will still have time to get your favorite coffee drink to help you start your day, all depends on finding those keys. After ten minutes of searching and finally having uncovered your keys, you now drive away in a stressed out and grumpy frame of mind.

Not a great way to start your day. In fact, you might feel as if your whole day has turned into a downward spiral, and your expectation is that the day is only going to get worse.

This experience channels your attitude into a negative funnel, which now colors every event that happens throughout the day. Not to mention, you are likely feeling stressed because you are arriving late now. There is no room or time for you to pause and take a breath or get that first cup of coffee. You don't give yourself an opportunity to reset your mindset.

So, therefore, let's take a moment to talk about how the application of the word *predictability* can actually help to destress these situations or even stop them from happening altogether.

Here is the result of using just the first step of *4 Simple Words*, that of *predictability*.

Starting Out Right

In the morning, when you come downstairs, you effortlessly pick up your car keys from the same place you always put them. You can predict with 100% certainty that they will be there. There wasn't 10 minutes of stressful searching, and your mindset is much calmer. You have time to get or make your favourite morning beverage. Then it is just a matter of getting into your car and driving off. Your day has now started in a simple, stress-free way. The rest of your commute will feel much smoother, simply because you didn't start out in a stressed frame of mind. You arrive on time, and you spend the day in a positive frame of mind. That small habit of predictability, which you created by simply putting your keys in the exact same place every day, immediately simplified your morning routine and kept your stress level low, while positively impacting your mood for the rest of the day.

Understanding the power of having more predictable actions in your life, can be empowering. It will mean a life more organized than previously, with increased efficiency. The *4 Simple Words* system's strength lies in its application. It boils down to first stepping out of your *comfort zone*, creating new habits and using some self-discipline, until those new, positive habits become automatic for you. If you find yourself needing some more help in establishing this new step, then I am here to coach you through it. Just go to: www.GettingOutFromUnderBook.com/Coaching.

Can you think of a few places throughout your day where that level of predictability could serve you well? Think about your morning routine for a start. You can probably identify two or three things that you are constantly searching for every morning, which add a hiccup of stress before you even walk out the door.

Have you ever felt that all you are constantly doing is putting out fires, with no time to plan ahead? Does your daily routine always feel as if you are behind, before you even walk out the door? Does that lack of predictability bleed into your professional life?

The thing to do then is to apply the step of "Predictability" into your life.

In fact, whenever you feel that things are getting out of your control, stop for a second, examine your situation, and ask yourself, "What can I do to make a part of this more predictable for the future, so that I can gain some control over it?" This will immediately simplify and calm things down for yourself.

As a simple exercise for yourself, break down your day. Be specific about the tasks that need to be completed, both large and small. Now look for ways to add more predictability into them. Go back and look at your morning routine as an example:

- Are there specific items that you need every morning?
- Are they located in one spot, or scattered throughout the house?
- Do you find yourself wasting valuable time looking for items, simply because they are never in the same place twice?
- Are there activities that have you taking multiple extra trips into different areas of the house, because related items are not all in the same place? (Think specifically of your morning getting-ready routine.)

While I specifically focused on your morning routine, because it sets the tone for your day, the truth is that you can take this examination for predictable elements into all times of your day, both personal and professional.

> *"Rather than cursing your fate, instead of empty wishes, act to make a difference. Be willing to change and go in a direction that leaves the problem far behind."*
>
> **Ralph Marston,** author of The Daily Motivator

As a further example, based in your professional world, what if you have been unexpectedly asked again to attend three meetings in the next two days, as well as get all your regular work done? This is when you can stop the overwhelm cycle in its tracks and take a moment to apply the first step in *4 Simple Words*: Predictability. Think about what actions you can take that will calm down the stress of this new situation, and still allow you to get all your work done. What can you delegate, or who can assist you?

Look for actions or steps that can be turned into predicable ones, especially for future situations like this, which is key to leaving the fog of confused, unclear thinking behind.

> **CALL TO ACTION**
>
> - Take a moment and write down one recent instance where you felt that the demand on your time was more than you could manage comfortably.
> - Now take that occasion and write down when and how you could have applied more predictability in this instance to create an easier, less stressful task.
>
> *If you feel that you are really ready to tackle a more involved uncluttering process for your life, then there is an online Extension Course that takes a more thorough and in-depth walk through the "Call To Action" steps, and much more!*
> Go to: www.GettingOutFromUnderBook.com

In the next few pages, I will explain the mechanics involved in creating less stress for yourself. Part of learning how to gain control in your life is to understand all the different parts that directly affect how your life functions on a daily basis.

This is a "**Motivational Moment**" that one of my clients told me one day:

"Whenever I am starting to feel that things are getting to be too much, and I am starting to feel overwhelmed, I hear your voice in my head. You say, 'Ask yourself what you can make more predictable with what you

are doing now, and then implement that.' So, I do that, and things start to feel better, and my anxiety reduces."

– Kleo Tobias, Fiber Art Educator and Presenter

The effect from having more predictable actions in your life, is increased simplicity, and when life becomes simple, then stress just drops away. It is the formula that has been used for years by my clients to gain a happier lifestyle.

The Quest for More Time

I am sure in the past you have tried various solutions in the hope they will give you more time, and they have failed you. If you are looking to have a dependable solution that will help you to create more time in your life to get things done, then your application of increasing more predictable actions or habits into it, is the solution you have been looking for.

It may seem at first glance like a small, insignificant point, but as I mentioned earlier, the difference between your wasting time and having mounting feelings of frustration can be found in procrastination and the lack of applying this single word, *predictability*. The additional reasons as to how you have ended up in your specific situation will be revealed further in this book.

What Successful People Do

All of us have the exact same 24 hours in any given day, yet some accomplish more than others within that same time frame. Why? Successful people know and use the power of predictability to their advantage. Experts, such as Olympic athletes and professional musicians, all practice for hours to gain predictability on their own actions so that they have less surprises and more certainty on reaching their goals.

> *"One important key to success is confidence. An important key to confidence is preparation."*
>
> **Arthur Ashe Jr.**, former number one professional tennis player in the world

The more times you repeat an action, the more certain and confident you become in its outcome. That predictability will help you feel more in control, and will decrease your stress and anxiety as you deal with all the demands on your time and energy, both personally and professionally. Through the use of my time-tested system, you can end your 24-hour day, feeling more accomplished and that you made progress as well, no matter how small it might be.

One of the positive aspects of predictability is that it can help contribute to an increased level of simplicity. Let's explore how that simplicity will serve to reduce your stress and allow you to live your best life, the one you have always had in your head but have not accomplished yet.

Chapter 3

THE POWER OF SIMPLICITY

As mentioned earlier in Chapter one, the word *simplicity* comes from the word *simple,* meaning *easily understood or done; presenting no difficulty.*

How many times have you asked yourself, "Where did my day go?" or "I haven't accomplished much today." So, you make the decision that the only solution to getting ahead is to work longer hours, and maybe bring some work home to work on late into the night, believing and hoping that it will increase your productivity. Using complex "solutions" like that is not the correct answer. It is also not sustainable, as eventually your physical and mental health will deteriorate because you are not taking care of yourself properly.

One of the definitions of simplicity is *freedom from complexity or intricacy.*

> "Successful people are simply those with successful habits."
>
> **Brian Tracy,** Canadian-American motivational public speaker and author

When I am coaching my clients to understand and gain clarity on this point, I often give this example. I hope this helps you too. If you wake up tired and are late for work in the morning (again), you immediately start to feel rushed and stressed, anticipating the day ahead. You skip breakfast because there is no time for that. When lunch rolls around, you gobble something unsatisfying at your desk, as you continue to struggle to address a backlog that never seems to end.

Halfway through the afternoon, you are falling asleep at your desk, because you were up way too late working the night before. So, you grab the nearest energy booster (aka, sugar rush) to help you make it through to the end of the day. However, you have lost track of time and got so immersed in what you were doing that you leave your office late. You suddenly realize that you have now missed leaving on time to pick up your daughter at her after-school activity.

Sound familiar?

Your tension mounts as you phone around, desperately trying to find someone to run over to the school and pick her up, because even if you left everything on your desk and raced out the door, you would still not make it on time. You also know you will receive that dirty look for being late yet again. You feel guilty about forgetting the time and not picking her up, annoyed with yourself that you are now further indebted to a friend who has responded to your plea for help to pick your daughter up for you. As you race home, the growing list of things you forgot expands, because you have no idea what to make for dinner. In fact, there is nothing in the house, because you were supposed to have done the grocery shopping. Now you have the added unexpected expense of picking up takeout food for dinner.

Your level of panic, the feelings of being overwhelmed, and the effect of life around you, continue to grow as you turn into a fast food restaurant to order dinner. Internally, you are thinking about what a failure you are at running your life, and you have no idea how to change it, except to bring home extra work yet again. The hope is that somehow working late into the night, after everyone is sleeping, will allow you to finally get ahead, in the hope that by some miracle, tomorrow will be different, and better. The pattern is now set, and so it continues day after day.

Does this example sound familiar? Were you nodding your head, recognizing pieces of your daily routine? If so, then you understand how futile this routine is, and why it needs to change.

The definition of insanity is doing the same thing over and over again, expecting a different result. The statistics confirm that approaching a problem with a complicated solution, such as working longer hours into the night, is going to fail 99% of the time. It is simply not sustainable.

It has been found, interestingly enough, that most people can only sustain an hour of consistent work without taking some type of break. In fact, many top successful athletes, CEOs, authors, and musicians never dedicate more than five hours consistently per day to their craft.

Food for thought?

Many top leaders recommend the 80–20 rule, where you work for 80% of the time (per hour) and then do something totally different for the other 20% of the time. They have found that this re-energizes them when they return to their work. Often, they come back with a new perspective, and enthusiasm as well.

To gain a better understanding of the effects of procrastination, clutter, and a lack of organization or personal time management, ask yourself the questions below:

- Do I feel refreshed when I wake up?
- Does most of my day feel relaxed, or stressed and overwhelming?

- Do I buy supplies, only to find out I already have them?
- Does it take me a long time to fall asleep at night?
- Do I not take time out to enjoy those people that have meaning in my life?
- Am I constantly feeling that no matter what I do, I can never catch up?
- Have I missed appointments that were important?
- Do I live in a chaotic, random, cluttered environment?
- Do I eat on the go, or take some time to stop and actually enjoy my meals?
- Am I in debt?
- Are my relationships suffering because I am more impatient than I used to be?

If you answered "Yes" to fifty percent or more of these questions, then you are already being adversely affected by clutter, chaos, stress, and unpredictable actions, along with a good amount of procrastination.

This being the case, you need proven tools, such as *4 Simple Words—predictability, simplicity,* and *stress relief*—to help you gain control of your life. You now have dependable tools that you can use anywhere to counter the complexity of your life with *simplicity*.

If your mind and physical spaces are cluttered, then you will not be able to make clear distinctions on what is truly essential and of importance in your life. Confusion, procrastination, and lack of focus all stem from clutter build-up, and prevent *simplicity* from occurring.

The Complexities of Life

The opposite of simplicity is *complexity*. In business, complexity only increases costs and reduces your profit margins as more complexity enters. The most desirable strategy then for business (and personal life) is *simplicity*. To state the obvious, to be simple is the most powerful way to be focused and productive.

Once you have a higher percentage of simplicity in your life, a soothing rhythm starts to enter into your daily routine. The natural end result of living a greatly simplified life is that you can experience more *stress relief* and increased happiness, as well as being more *present* or *in the moment*.

Now that is a really great end-goal to aim for!

In other words, the more predictable actions you put into your life, the simpler life becomes, and consequently your stress level reduces in direct relation to this sequence.

CALL TO ACTION

- Pick a tool or piece of equipment you use often and locate where it is.
- Where is the place it is supposed to live?
- Is it in good working order? If so, then place it where it is supposed to live, in a spot convenient to you.
- Now go into action and do the same step with five more tools or pieces of equipment that you use all the time that are not where they are supposed to be.
- Creating more predictable steps like these will help you to stop burning up your valuable time searching for things you need in the future. You will also increase your ability to focus, which will enable you to increase your personal efficiency, productivity, and success in life.

If you feel that you are really ready to tackle a more involved uncluttering process for your life, then there is an online Extension Course that takes a more thorough and in-depth walk through the "Call To Action" steps, and much more!

Go to: www.GettingOutFromUnderBook.com

Now go into action, and make sure you have created permanent spaces for your tools or equipment to live in, which you can easily find in the future.

Once you apply these steps in your life, you will also gain focus, which will enable you to increase your personal efficiency, productivity, and success in life.

> *"A place for everything and everything in its place."*
> **Samuel Smiles**, Scottish author; taken from his essay, "Thrift"

The Golden Timer to the Rescue!

Grab an egg timer or use the timer on your phone. This is now what you call your *Golden Timer*. I call it *golden* because it is golden what this simple little device can do for your ability to establish good habits in your life, and to get things done that you have been putting off.

The idea here is to enable you to get things completed with more ease. However, that will not happen at the beginning if you put the timer on for too long a period of time, especially at the beginning. *Do not go over one hour.* Take smaller bites at the task you are trying to complete. I suggest you start with ten minutes.

I think there must be a graph somewhere that shows that the longer you have not done some task, the longer you think it will take to actually get it done. Any task you have been putting off for some time will seem larger and grow more overwhelming in your mind, the longer you push it off into the realm of procrastination—a "strange but true" concept.

For Example: Yes, the task of uncluttering the garage is a big task that will take many hours, and the thought of doing that in one go is overwhelming. I understand, but this is exactly when you need to use the Golden Timer (same applies for sorting receipt and tax filings or writing a report you have been putting off).

Nibbling Your Way to Success!

Your "I'll do it later" procrastinated task will quickly become the "elephant in your room"—at home or at work. This is that one thing in your life that is not looked at or talked about—or is avoided completely until it becomes so overwhelming you can think of nothing else. It seems to grow bigger as time goes by and you continue to persist in your avoidance of it.

You need to confront this elephant to make it disappear, but the question is . . . How?

A children's joke goes like this:

Question: How do you eat an elephant so you can reduce it or get rid of it?

Answer: One bite or one nibble at a time!

By putting The Golden Timer on for small bites of time (ten, twenty, thirty minutes at a time), you can nibble away gradually on a task until it (the elephant in the room) is completely gone, and you are freed at last from the stressful feeling that has overwhelmed you about that previously procrastinated task.

Here is another example on how The Golden Timer can help you:

I love a clean house but hate cleaning, so I regularly put it off. Every time I think about it, in my mind, I believe it will take me even more time to clean than previously thought.

So, I use The Golden Timer. No, I am not one of those women that get joy out of cleaning their house. Instead, my thoughts go immediately to all the other things I could be doing that do not involve cleaning.

Don't get me wrong; I love a clean space, but I just have no excitement on being the one to get it to that state. So, in my mind, because I do not like to do this task, I would first put it off as long as I can. Then I would decide that it is going to take me hours to do "blah" cleaning. Of course, I knew I did not have hours of free time to devote to this, as I am busy running my businesses and working with clients. So, naturally, I decided that it needed to be put off for another time.

Once I put on the timer and actually started cleaning, I was amazed at what little time it actually took to get it done, compared to what I had developed in my head as how long it would take.

Implementing the use of The Golden Timer has stopped all my procrastination and mental gymnastics, along with my justifications for why I should not clean the house. As one of my clients has said to me, *"The Golden Timer is the greatest thing since sliced bread, and like a loaf of bread, you eat it one bite at a time."*

It also allowed me to understand and have a better grasp of reality of knowing the real length of time it took to get that task accomplished. Knowing how long something takes to get done can be very helpful, in the office or other environments in your life. The Golden Timer is a valuable tool to have in your tool kit of life.

The Benefits You Gain From Using The Golden Timer

- As time is inclined to get distorted when you have taken a long time to confront something (such as sorting tax receipts, papers, filing, cleaning, etc.), The Golden Timer can teach you how long a particular task will take to do, and give you a base line for future tasks.
- In addition, it can help you to establish new positive habits in your life, and thereby a higher

percentage of the *4 Simple Words, predictability, simplicity,* and *stress relief*. After all, habits are the invisible architecture of our lives.

- Your confidence will grow as you accomplish more than you ever thought you could, all without stress, simply because you used The Golden Timer to tackle what you did not like to do. Just by nibbling it away . . .

Remember, take bite-sized pieces of time—your eyes can be bigger than your stomach at the beginning, when using The Golden Timer. I really cannot stress this enough to you; gradient steps are needed here. Do not demand too much of yourself at the beginning, or you will fail again.

The fact is that you ARE confronting whatever you have been putting off until now—so give yourself some compassion and take the slower but *Golden* road to success. Be kind to yourself.

Rules of the Game

For The Golden Timer to really work for you as expected, you need to adhere to the policy that goes along with The Golden Timer. Here it is:

- Exclusively and ONLY work on that single task that you set the timer for—no answering the phone, no emails, no playing on the computer, or with your family pet or child—nothing else until the buzzer goes off at the end.

- Put it on for any amount of time you like, but for not more than one hour. Best suggestion is for ten, twenty, or a maximum of thirty minutes, which is ideal unless you get a feeling of anxiety with that amount of time. Remember: take baby steps.

- When the timer goes off, walk away. Down tools! Go make some tea, go for a walk, etc. Do something different. You can always return to this at a later time. Take a break before you go "back in" for another go. If you work past The Golden Timer buzzer, you will start to *grind your gears*, get tired of the task, start to hate it, and never want to return to it ever again. In short, you have just overwhelmed yourself into apathy on ever getting this task done. So do not do this to yourself!

- Celebrate! It is really important that you celebrate or acknowledge to yourself that you actually went in and handled the hell out of this task for the "x" minutes you had the timer on for. Yes, there is more to be done, but you just did more than you have done in weeks, months, or even years. So, allow yourself the pride and success-thinking, that you DID DO SOMETHING ABOUT IT, and it felt good.

The application of The Golden Timer into your tasks will assist you greatly with your ability to focus, and to get things completed. This, in turn, will give you more time doing what brings you joy and satisfaction, which is another positive effect of a life simplified.

Breaking Free From Stress

The higher percentage of predictable action steps, along with the use of The Golden Timer, will immediately increase calmness in your life.

It's time to start getting rid of clutter and living your dreams, not living within your fears.

Chapter 4

WHAT HAS CLUTTER GOT TO DO WITH IT?

The relationship between physical clutter in your environment and your mental clutter has a major effect on your ability to function well or not. The connection is often greater than you even realize.

Incidents of anxiety and "panic" attacks are on the rise for a lot of people. As the fast-paced world around us increases, it can become emotionally overwhelming to keep on top of it all. The demand for your attention is incessant. As clutter builds and those demands collide, your mental and physical energy become drained and unfocused.

Dr. Meredith Marten, an assistant professor of anthropology at the University of West Florida (UWF), and a lead author of a study, in 2018, on the effects of stress, told Global News, "Experiences of chronic stress, which engage the human stress response, can lead over time to poor health outcomes, particularly cardiovascular conditions and immune suppression, among others."

With increased use of various demanding digital devices in your daily life, and the threat of environmental catastrophes looming, I am sure chronic stress, along with its poor health outcomes, is on the rise.

Your Comfort Zone

You have your own level of comfort when it comes to physical clutter (or mess), as does everyone else you know, whether it is clutter in the home or business life. For you, a pencil out of place might drive you crazy, while for others they have to be repeatedly tripping over a mound of pencils before they decide to reduce the cluttered mound of pencils in their way.

It is all a matter of personal perspective and tolerance. Knowing your own level of comfort is very helpful, especially if you are living with someone who has a different level of clutter comfort than you. As an aside to this, I have yet to find any two individuals living together to have identical levels of clutter-comfort. This makes for some interesting coaching scenarios, as you can imagine!

> *"The great courageous act that we must all do, is to have the courage to step out of our history and past so that we can live our dreams."*
>
> **Oprah Winfrey**, American media executive, talk show host, actress, television producer, and philanthropist

The Clutter Triangle

To be properly aware of what you are up against, you first need to understand the mechanics involved. You need to know that there are actually three types of clutter. These are mental, physical, as well as virtual (electronic/digital) clutter, which can be directly affecting your ability to function, focus, and accomplish tasks successfully.

The Physical Side of Things

In fact, the physical clutter that you put out of your line of vision doesn't mean that the mental stress on you from that clutter has disappeared. It might actually be worse, simply because you now worry about your clutter unexpectedly being uncovered by another from the place you have been hiding it.

Definition – Physical clutter: A collection of things lying about in an untidy mass; a jumble; disorder; something or some things that do not have a place to be or location where they actually belong.

We all have some level of clutter in our physical spaces. For example, the snail-mail keeps arriving and piling up in the kitchen, and the spare room or basement has been turned into a storage dumping ground for things you do not know what to do with or have procrastinated on.

Your solution to just stuff the papers into a drawer or simply shut the door to the spare room or basement, where you have "temporarily" dumped them, does not cause them to magically vanish. Out of sight does not always mean out of mind.

The longer you wait for these things to miraculously disappear on their own, the more they pile up and start creeping into more and more of your space. The longer your clutter collection builds, the harder it is for you to concentrate and really focus. All the while, your feelings of stress and anxiety build, as your fear of others finding out about your clutter collection and judging you harshly builds. Eventually, you feel so overwhelmed by it all that just thinking about it becomes too much.

Over the years, through my coaching clients, I have observed for myself how the relationship of too much physical clutter in one's own space has a direct detrimental effect on one's ability to function clearly mentally. When your physical clutter has passed your personal comfort zone, your focus becomes fragmented, and this then opens the door to rising anxiety and increasing stress and overwhelm for yourself. The resulting effect of this creates more and more mental clutter for you to try and battle through. Simply put, as your procrastination builds past your own clutter comfort zone barrier, you become overwhelmed by it all.

CALL TO ACTION: (Physical Clutter)

- What area in your immediate physical environment (at business or at home) could do with some uncluttering actions?
- Write down the first area that immediately comes to your mind.
- You can put bags or boxes in the area labelled for charity, re-gifting, garbage, or re-homing or keeping. Use these to assist you to unclutter your physical space; it will help you.
- Work through the area, decluttering bit by bit.
- Now go into action and do the same step with three more spaces that are bothering you and can do with some uncluttering.
- Now write down how you felt before you did this exercise.
- Take a moment to check on yourself and write down how you feel now that you have reduced some of your physical clutter.

If you feel that you are really ready to tackle a more involved uncluttering process for your life, then there is an online Extension Course that takes a more thorough and in-depth walk through the "Call To Action" steps, and much more!

Go to: www.GettingOutFromUnderBook.com

Defining the Mental Side of Things

Definition – Mental Clutter: A confused or disordered state; a lessened ability to concentrate, and a higher state of stress, often accompanied by sleeplessness.

Mental clutter is identifiable by your scattered attention, along with a complete inability to focus consistently on a single task for an extended period of time. As well, you will have a lessened ability to fully complete any task.

The feeling of confusion, an increase in forgetfulness and overwhelm, accompanied by an increase in procrastination as well as stress levels, are all symptoms of mental clutter. These effects are proof that you have been trying to hold too much information in your mind at one time. This is what we call mental clutter.

> **CALL TO ACTION: (Mental clutter)**
>
> - Identify one thing that you can stop storing in your head, and then write down one way you can immediately reduce your mental clutter.
> - Work through this one thing by downloading whatever you have been holding onto in your head and put it onto paper or a document in your computer. Just get it out of your head.
> - Creating a new mental uncluttering policy on how you will put the step you just did into action on a regular basis, releasing them from your mind onto paper or a document on the computer, is very helpful.
> - Now go into action and do the same step with three more things that are cluttering your mind and are bothering you.
> - Now write down how you felt before you did this exercise.
> - Take a moment to check on yourself and write down how you feel now that you have reduced some of your mental clutter.
>
> *If you feel that you are really ready to tackle a more involved uncluttering process for your life, then there is an online Extension Course that takes a more thorough and in-depth walk through the "Call To Action" steps, and much more!*
>
> *Go to: www.GettingOutFromUnderBook.com*

The third type of clutter has actually increased over the years as we all become more dependent on our electronics, for both our business and personal lives.

Buzz, Buzz, Whiz, Whiz

> **Definition – Virtual or Electronic Clutter:** Too many electronic devices accumulated, which are being used all at once or continuously; an accumulation of electronic information that is past its usefulness.

The constant demand for your attention from anything that beeps, pings, buzzes, or whizzes, can wear you down and increase your anxiety, because you feel you are missing something important by not responding instantly to it. Add to this the build-up of unanswered emails and texts accumulating in your IN baskets, and you have electronic clutter.

To Cell or Not to Cell—That is the Question!

Some of my clients have created daily cell-free times by switching off their cell phone for one or two hours, thereby creating a pool of tranquility for themselves, enabling them to rejuvenate without interruption. They found it to be an emotionally freeing experience. Try it and see how freeing this one action can be for you. Try it just for fifteen or thirty minutes at the beginning to see how you feel.

Cell phone addiction. I see problems with cell phone use in many of my clients. I understand you were never given any etiquette or policy on when and how to use your phone. But regardless, there are certain good phone behaviours I suggest you adopt, to make your life smoother.

CALL TO ACTION: (Electronic clutter)

- Here are just three basic key actions you can take in keeping electronic clutter from building up and overwhelming you.

- Get into the habit of switching your phone off for part of each day. Give yourself a mental break from the onslaught of unrelenting communication and demands for answers from you.

- Switch it off when in a meeting, family gathering, or out for a meal. Get involved in what is right in front of you in real life. Showing respect and consideration for others time is just common good manners.

- Let others know that you have a cut off time in the evening for any calls, particularly for business calls, texts, and emails. Let them know that if they arrive after your time deadline, you will attend to them the next day. Be steadfast on this. Protect your private time, as this will decrease stress and allow you to decompress from the day and to simplify your life.

- Just as you do with emails on your computer, clean out your phone of texts, emails, old apps, and games you no longer use. Delete photos you no longer want, if not every week or month, then at least every quarter of the year.

The Invaders Are Here!

Most people, like you, have no idea what to do with all the digital clutter that constantly invades their life. Add to that your lack of action on deleting files and emails or storing them in an insecure manner, and your personal or business information is at risk. On top of this, the storage capacity of your devices increases practically with each upgrade, and you have quickly lost control of a part of your life.

To illustrate my point, experts have said recently that all our technology, along with cyber bullying, has added another layer to young people's stress. All this technology is affecting their ability to focus and relax. One expert was quoted as saying, "A lot of young people are having difficulty maintaining their attention span because they're always looking to see what's coming through on social media."

There is also some recent research that talks about how children who are constantly looking at their phones, and who are being bombarded with continual information, are structurally changing their brain. The experts say that this action, due to the background noise, actually prevents them from relaxing and being more mindful. That, in turn, makes them feel stressed.

I am sure you can recall a time when you struggled and failed to find something digitally that you needed, and how that frustrated you.

So, when exactly was the last time that you searched for a particular document or email and could not find it?

I thought so.

In December 2018, Professor Darshana Sedera, of

Monash University, Australia, presented a paper that he and co-author, Dr. Sachithra Lokuge, also of Monash University, had written. It described how they surveyed 846 people about digital hoarding habits, as well as the levels of stress they felt. They discovered that there was a link between digital hoarding behaviours and levels of stress participants reported.

How many times have you opened your IN box to find it full, and your computer is screaming for even more space, because of all the photos, games, and endless list of scanned documents that you have convinced yourself are necessary to keep? Does this relax you or increase your stress level?

With that in mind, I want you to start focusing on simplifying your digital life.

Interrupting Your Flow

You can start by setting up a new policy for yourself on what times of day you will reply to your emails each day. You should not be answering them all day long just because they ping at you to let you know they have arrived in your IN box. Every time you interrupt yourself by checking your In Box or text, you have fractured your focus on what you were doing previously, and it takes a long time to fully be present in returning to what you were doing before they pinged at you.

When doing the Call to Action, just go back one month of time from right now. Going back further may put you into an overwhelmed mindset, so do not do that.

CALL TO ACTION: (Electronic – General)

- These electronic uncluttering actions will help you to feel less anxiety, and clearer mentally.
- Go to your computer and erase 40 old emails you no longer need or want, going back just one month from today. Be honest with yourself. Don't fall for the excuses or justifications that you have allowed in the past.
- Go to your phone and erase any old texts that you no longer need or want, going back one month from today. They can be promotion texts, or appointment confirmation texts for your dental appointment, etc.
- Create a new policy for yourself as to when you will answer your emails and texts during the day, and when, in the future, you will take the time to unclutter your electronic storage, starting two months back from now.
- Now write down how you felt before you did this exercise.
- Take a moment to check on yourself and write down how you feel now that you have actually reduced some of your electronic clutter.

If you feel that you are really ready to tackle a more involved uncluttering process for your life, then there is an online Extension Course that takes a more thorough and in-depth walk through the "Call To Action" steps, and much more!

Go to: www.GettingOutFromUnderBook.com

If you know how to put an alarm on your phone or computer, or use a physical calendar, then do so for the next time you have planned to electronically unclutter.

When you have too much clutter (of any type), any free time you thought you had, will be gone. So, unclutter your way to a better life!

"Forever" Storage Mentality

If you are struggling with your electronic clutter, and it seems almost paralyzing to even consider pushing that delete button, you are not alone.

The next chapter discusses a growing problem, one that involves your digital devices and how unlimited storage is negatively impacting your ability to clear the clutter and simplify. Read on . . .

Chapter 5

THE GROWING EPIDEMIC

Digital hoarding is defined as "the accumulation of digital files to the point of loss of perspective, which eventually results in stress and disorganisation." It has even been suggested that it might be a new subtype of a hoarding disorder.

Wikipedia defines digital hoarding (also known as e-hoarding or cyber hoarding) as "excessive acquisition and reluctance to delete electronic material no longer valuable to the user." That excess digital media is often referred to as "digital clutter," just as physical build-up is described as "clutter" or "junk."

- When you open up your computer, is it covered with folders and pages covering the entire surface?
- Do you get a feeling of rising stress or a feeling of overwhelm happening when you first open up your computer to work on something?

- When was the last time that you spent thirty minutes searching for something on your electronic device, which you had carefully stored for later, and then given up because you simply couldn't find it?

If any of these have ever happened to you, then you might be stuck in a cycle of cyber hoarding.

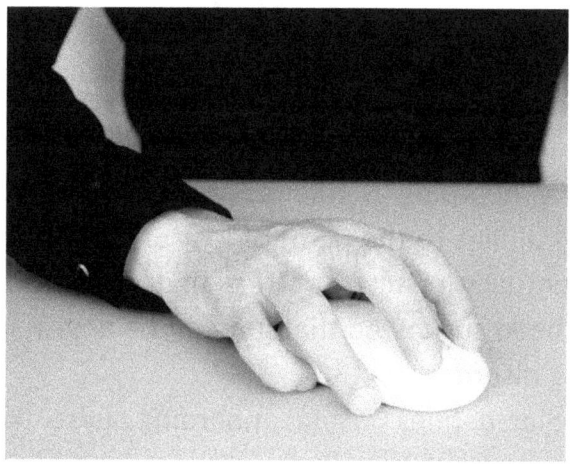

I am here to tell you that if your appetite for information far exceeds the time that you have to consume it all, you are not the only person storing too much data on your laptop or phone. In fact, this is a digital epidemic that is having its impact on health, wellness, productivity, and interpersonal relationships worldwide.

So why then do you turn your life into a digital dumping ground? One reason is that due to the constant demand for decision-making these days, it is more pleasant to put off the decision making on what to do with "it," and easier to just store "it" *for later*.

Unlike a physical hoarder, who is limited by the four walls and square footage that he or she has to store stuff, there are infinite digital storage options available, including infinite Cloud storage. So, for a digital hoarder, the storage capacity is literally limitless.

Digital hoarding has now been labelled as a psychiatric disorder. Just as physical hoarding fills your home with stuff to an overwhelming negative effect on you mentally, so too does the over storage of digital clutter impact your memory, your focus, and your ability to concentrate.

Why is it that the technologies that were designed for us to foster connectedness, and strengthen relationships, seems to be producing the opposite effect? Human detachment and loneliness are on the rise and have been sighted as some of the side effects from our unique electronic age. Along with that, there is the rise in teenage suicide, panic attacks, and an overall increase of anxiety issues. In other words, our technological advances can be intimidating as well as overwhelming.

It is overwhelming.

I am sure that you have previously wasted time going down what I call, "the digital rabbit hole." For example, when your friend sends you a random piece of information. Maybe it is a picture of a tiger. So, you download the lovely tiger photo, along with the plan in your head to look at it again, later. Then you get curious as to where tigers come from. This question leads you to look up information about tigers, which then leads you to the country of China, and now you are interested in learning about China itself.

Now your curiosity has been peaked on what they eat there. Perhaps you download a sheet with basic questions and answers on China and their cultural eating habits, which you also plan to read, later.

As you skim that sheet before filing it away, you notice that Chinese love to eat noodles, but you thought that noodles actually came from Italy. Now you are hunting down information regarding the origin of noodles and how Italy got the noodles that are such a fundamental part of their culture. A quick search and now you have another picture and information sheet about Marco Polo, the explorer who brought noodles from China, to file away for you to read, later.

Now you have lost all track of time. Plus, you have forgotten what you initially got online to hunt for in the first place, before you dove down the endless information rabbit hole—time wasted, procrastination in full operation, as you add to your "later" collection of digital overwhelm.

If you don't think that constantly saving information for later, and overloading yourself digitally, is not impacting your life, think again.

> *"In order to be happy, human beings must feel they are continuing to grow. Clearly, we must adopt the concept of continuous improvement as a daily principle."*
> **Tony Robbins**, American author, motivational life coach, and philanthropist

Breaking the Digital Hoarding Habit

As mentioned earlier, in Chapter 4, start breaking this negative habit by creating a new policy for yourself on how often you will delete your data, and then stick to that policy without making excuses to yourself. Google is a great tool that allows you to find information again if you need it after you have deleted it. Nothing is truly gone forever in the electronic world, so holding onto these is just cluttering your life without improving its overall quality.

On a regular basis (I suggest weekly), sort through your emails, deleting all the old and answered emails. I also encourage you to go through the various programs that you have, and delete what you no longer use, be it music, stored recipes, videos, or any other attachments. Truthfully, thanks to subscription services and Google, you can always find anything again, if you decide you want to revisit them at a later date.

Before you dismiss these suggestions and argue that you do not have a problem with the effects of digital overwhelm, I want to share a few statistics that might open your eyes to your digital habits.

There are some disturbing stats, compiled some time ago by Trend Micro, a cyber security company that hopefully will give you second thoughts about your own e-hoarding tendencies:

- 52% of users claim the items on their computers are irreplaceable, even though they typically only use 20% of what they save.

- Around 2.8 years of financial information is stored on computers.
- An average user has 65 apps installed on his/her smartphone but only uses 15.
- Americans send an average of 582 text messages per month.
- An average Facebook user has 229 friends, 16 of whom he/she doesn't personally know.
- An average Twitter user has 126 followers, only 35% of whom are real people.
- More than 60 million photos are added to Facebook each week.
- More than 60 photos are added to Instagram each second.
- More than 60 hours of videos are uploaded to YouTube each minute.
- Around 190 million tweets are sent each day.

Yup, time to clean up your e-hoarding habits!

Dr. Darshana Sedera, internationally recognized leader in the field of innovation, enterprise social media, outsourcing and enterprise systems, says from one of his studies, "What we found was actually, in the digital space, unknowingly or knowingly, we all are sort of entering into that stressful state."

For example, when you ask a physical hoarder why it is so difficult for them to let go of their "stuff," their answer is exactly the same that digital hoarders say about their emails, photos, and texts: "Well, it might be useful in the future."

Sound familiar?

Justifications given for hanging onto emails range from laziness, thinking something might come in handy later, or an increase in anxiety over the idea of deleting anything, or wanting to keep "ammunition" against someone. You talk yourself into believing that all the digital information you have collected is going to end up needing to be produced for someone at a future date.

Now, I am not saying, because you store too many emails, photos, and texts, that you should classify yourself as a digital hoarder. I am suggesting, however, that you are creating negative habits identical to hoarders, and that if allowed to continue, it cannot end well for you. Eventually, it will add another layer to your stress and feelings of being overwhelmed. Clutter, no matter the form, can really impact you negatively.

The Concern about Your Emails

This same research team of Dr. Darshana Sedera and Dr. Sachithra Lokuge, mentioned previously, assessed digital hoarding behaviours in the workplace. They tested 203 people who used computers as part of their job. What they found was that concern for emails, above all other digital technologies, appears to be a particular problem among participants. The average inbox had 102 unread, and 331 read, emails.

Instead of giving yourself a hard time for taking too many selfies or having too many unread emails and texts, just try reducing the problem. Start by erasing any unwanted and unnecessary electronic clutter as they arrive, or at least erase them once a week or once a month, or in a worst-case scenario, once a quarter.

When exactly was the last time you cleaned out your email IN basket or photos?

The problem with digital clutter is that just like any other type of clutter, it makes finding anything challenging. Plus, once those search results are returned, you will likely spend valuable time weeding through them to find the one you really want. To clarify this for yourself, take a moment and add up all the time you have spent searching for emails or other digital records in the last week. Seems like a large waste of time, doesn't it?

Let's talk about how predictability and simplicity can work in your favor just to help you manage your digital storage. The point here is to keep what is important and make it easy to locate. Creating a set of rules for your emails can be one way to have your inbox sorted automatically.

Imagine how much relief it can give you just to have the incoming digital clutter handled. This will help to reduce your stress and anxiety, right now. Doing so will make it easier for you to start tackling those next critical steps in your desire for a better life.

CALL TO ACTION

- These electronic uncluttering actions will help you to feel less anxiety and be mentally clearer and more focused.

- Create one archive folder (physical or electronic) where you want to store (your minimal) email information you think you might have need of down the road. By this, I mean for you to be VERY cutthroat as to what you feel needs to be stored. It can be personal or business.

- In addition to this (per your recent policy decision), I recommend that once every week or month, you evaluate these stored archive emails to see if they still need to continue to be stored or can be erased.

- Go to your contact list, either on your phone or your computer, and erase all contacts you do not recognise or need.

- Do the same action with 20–40 of your stored photos. If you are ruthless with yourself, then you will see how you do not need 10 photos of Aunt Mary on the last vacation to remind you of that time. You just need one or two. So, cull those photos or print them, and thereby end the cycle of "forever storage."

- Continue to unclutter in any other electronic device collection you may have.

- If you have not already put an electronic alarm on your phone or computer for the next time you have scheduled the spring cleaning of your unwanted electronic data, then do so now. If you are not sure how to do this, then you can use a paper calendar to mark down the next date of digital erasure.
- Now write down how you felt before you did this exercise.
- Take a moment to check on yourself and write down how you feel now that you have actually reduced some of your stored "for later" electronic clutter.

If you feel that you are really ready to tackle a more involved uncluttering process for your life, then there is an online Extension Course that takes a more thorough and in-depth walk through the "Call To Action" steps, and much more!

Go to: www.GettingOutFromUnderBook.com

Dealing with your incoming clutter can help you to reclaim time on a daily basis and give you the ability to breathe without constantly feeling overwhelmed.

Simplicity Itself!

If you want more time in your day to do the things that make you happy and fulfill your soul, then the equation is simplicity itself. Learn to become more efficient with your time by increasing your personal time management skills and use the tools in this book to help you with that.

It is best to start by eliminating your immediate physical clutter and chaos, by applying the principles of those *4 Simple Words*. Increased predictability on where things can be found immediately, will be the foundation on which to build your future success.

This is a "**Motivational Moment**":

"Jeannette's knowledge and expertise is much appreciated in reorganizing our company structure. Just after a couple of meetings, the organizational chart took shape the way I want it. Her 4 Simple Words system, and the use of The Golden Timer, have really helped to make things less stressful. She is very professional and caring and ensured that I did not go down the time-wasting rabbit-hole, so I can now focus towards reaching my goals!"

Naveed Hyder, Founder and Principal Designer, www.h5interiors.com

Chapter 6

THE DEADLIEST OF DISEASES

Just stop stopping yourself!

Understanding what it is exactly that prevents you from getting all the things done that you need to do is key. After all, if you are going to clear the blocks that are keeping you stuck and feeling overwhelmed, you have to first identify them. Once you do, then you can strategize the best methods with which to address those blocks, utilizing the tools and strategies that you will find throughout this book.

But before you do this, I want you to a take a moment and ask yourself why you want to de-stress and create more time. What is your reason for improving your life emotionally and financially? What is your passion? What or who is important to you in your life? What ideal dream image do you have of how you envisioned your life to become one day? Write down a list of all the people and places and things that are the reasons you want to get out from overwhelm and be successful in your life. It might be a good idea to also list out what your definition of real success means to you. Is it having more money, having lots of free time to spend with your loved ones, or only working a few days a week? List them out.

Now that you know your reasons for improving your life, one of the first blocks that most of us have, contributing to our clutter and feelings of stress and frustration, is procrastination.

The definition of **procrastination**, as I mentioned earlier, is "The action of delaying or postponing something, or putting off or delaying, especially something requiring immediate attention." The more you understand the problem, the easier it will be for you to conquer it once and for all. With less procrastination in your life, the happier, calmer, and less overwhelmed you will become.

As *New York Times* best-selling author, Raymond Aaron, points out in his book, *Double Your Income Doing What You Love*, which was co-authored with Sue Lacher, there are two types of procrastinators: the Optimist Procrastinator, who believes he has enough time to get the task done, and so delays doing it until realization that his or her time has run out, and now has to go flat out, at the exclusion of everything else to complete the task. Then there is the Pessimist Procrastinator, who senses right from the start that there is no way the task assigned can get accomplished, for various reasons. It all boils down to you not wanting to do something, so you start the procrastinate habit.

Which one are you?

Why Your Time Disappears

Procrastination usually starts by you not wanting to make a decision or do a particular task. Is it your tax receipts, cleaning the house, cooking the food, writing up a particular report, that you hate doing? Do you consider it to be a chore, with no joy or satisfaction in it for you? If so, you put it off. I have observed over the years that the longer you put something off, the larger and more complex and uncomfortable, as well as time consuming, it appears to be in your mind. What originally would have taken twenty minutes, you now consider will take two hours, and well, you know you do not have two hours to spare on this, so you put it off again. Sound familiar? It certainly has to most of my clients.

If procrastination has become the bedrock of your life, it can become the single most chronic "illness" that holds you back and eats away your potential for success. The build-up of stress as you postpone each decision and task for "later," builds into an overwhelming sense of, "I have no time!"

Making decisions becomes so difficult that you just stop trying to make them altogether.

Your own inaction is factually what feeds this build-up of tension and confusion.

Part of the downside of chronic procrastination is that when you have been in this continuous negative state of overwhelm for a long time, it will impact your physical and mental health adversely. This self-created poor health situation can create an out of control deadly mix of stress and panic attacks that can lead to other health issues. You end up treating all those physical symptoms, but the original reasons for your ill health just gets ignored. Until now!

> *"We are what we repeatedly do. Excellence, then, is not an act but a habit."*
> **Aristotle,** Greek Philosopher, known as the "Father of Western Philosophy"

If you have been experiencing procrastination for a long time, then I suggest you contact a local Professional Organizer's Association, who can help you with this. They can help you to reverse this deadly mix of stress and ill health. However, if you feel you have sufficient motivation and discipline left to get yourself out of this self-created hole you have busily dug for yourself, then great! Start digging out and completing all your procrastinated tasks—now!

The Hard Truth of the Matter

It can be quite jarring to realize that it has been you, and you alone all along, who has actively been stopping yourself from having a happier life. But no worries—something can be done about it! Just keep reading and applying the information in this book. This is truly the best thing you can do to help yourself create more time in your life, investing in your future ideal successful lifestyle.

If you believe that time is money, then you need to understand that procrastination is the enemy of that time, and that your future success in both your private and professional life is at stake

For entrepreneurs with a small business, who are the boss of everything, procrastination along with poor personal time management skills can spell disaster. It can and will prevent your business from expanding stably, and even possibly cause it to implode. In a larger business, depending on the depth of the procrastination "disease" within it, the same can also occur. It lowers productivity and erases efficiency and effectiveness in what tasks need to get prioritized and accomplished first.

Your guide in successfully turning this dwindling, time wasting spiral around is to simply decide to have a policy where you do those important tasks "right now!" Or you can delegate them to someone else to get completed. That works too.

CALL TO ACTION

- What makes you happy? What brings a smile to your face and a feeling of satisfaction into your life?
- Write down one thing that gives you positive feelings in your life.
- Now write down what you need to do, so that you can experience this more frequently.
- Write down one thing that gives you a feeling of pressure or obligation, with no positive feelings, and causes you to feel trapped into *"I have to do this."*
- Now write out a proposed solution for it, where someone else can step in and do that thing you hate to do, instead of you always having to do it.
- Once a month, take one thing permanently off your "hate-to-do" list, and get it delegated.
- It does not always require money. You can barter with someone or ask a friend or family member for help.
- Now write down how you felt before you did this exercise.
- Take a moment to check on yourself, and write down how you feel now that you have actually identified one thing that you know you can do to make you happy, and one that you need to delegate.

> *If you feel that you are really ready to tackle a more involved uncluttering process for your life, then there is an online Extension Course that takes a more thorough and in-depth walk through the "Call To Action" steps, and much more!*
>
> *Go to: www.GettingOutFromUnderBook.com*

By doing these actions, you cut down your procrastination opportunities and create more time for a happier quality of life, doing more of what you love, and letting others do those tasks that drag you down and cause you to want to procrastinate.

Start by Establishing Your Foundation Stone

Learning how to use the power of more predictable actions in your life can be very rewarding and actually empowering. The *4 Simple Words* strength lies in its application. For some clarification on this, I have laid out for you some pros and cons of these small steps, to help you better understand the effect these four simple words can have on your life. Some may surprise you. Others will hopefully help to motivate you in continuing this journey of uncluttering and organizing.

Predictability equals gains for you:

- Less time wasted looking for things.
- You can immediately find what you are looking for, thereby saving yourself time and stress.
- Ability to plan ahead, establishing goals and, logically, step-by-step, working towards their attainment.
- Confidence builds, knowing where you are going and in exactly which direction to head, to accomplish your next goal.
- Because you plan ahead, you spend less time in the office or doing the tasks you need to do. In other words, you will become more efficient and economical with your time.
- Spending more time on things you love to do that enrich your life and soul.

Simplicity equals gains for you:

- Calmer personal and physical environments.
- Improved ability to focus, which will result in completing strategic steps of projects sooner and with more ease.
- Gain a more relaxed and confident air about yourself, reducing health risks.
- Increased ability to control your professional life.

- More mental and physical space as clutter is reduced.

Stress reduction and relief equals gains for you:

- Better, deeper, continuous sleep.
- Improved and strengthened health.
- Seamless focus to concentrate on successful steps of a plan, and certainty in the knowledge that things will work out for you.
- Greatly improved attitude towards life.
- Ability to really relax, guilt-free, openly enjoying those things that add value and meaning to your existence, the result of which is a much happier life!
- Successful professional and personal relationships, being able to be fully committed and living "in the moment."
- Peace

When you apply the steps from this book, you will discover that you have the tools to pull yourself out from under overwhelm in any situation. My intention is to give you a sense of personal empowerment for the rest of your life, enabling you to create a stable, happier future for yourself and those around you, at last.

Chapter 7

YES, YOUR HEALTH IS AT RISK

Throughout these chapters, there have been frequent mentions of stress, anxiety, and feelings of being overwhelmed. The obvious side effects from living with these things chronically are both physical and mental. A few of those obvious signs include high blood pressure, headaches, upset stomach, panic attacks, overindulgence and weight gain, to name a few. Your mind and body actually rebel at being caught in a constant cycle of stress.

When you are stressed, your body releases a hormone called cortisol, which when released over a prolonged length of time, can become a catalyst for a host of problems. Long-term stress and its effects on the body are fast becoming a serious drain on societies' health care systems.

To Sleep or Not to Sleep; That is the Question

Recent studies show that when you are lacking in sleep, it can cause you to crave sugar-based foods and snacks, which in turn can cause weight gain; and from that, of course, there comes a host of other health issues. So now you have additional reasons to de-stress your body and mind.

Acute Stress – The Fight or Flight Mechanism

You are constantly bombarded by threats and changes, but because you don't usually run away or actually fight, you stay in a reactive state. Consequently, you are bathed and flooded in stress hormones. After a stressful life event has passed, it takes about 90 minutes for your metabolism to return to normal (or to your previous state), prior to the perceived threat.

Chronic State

This day-to-day stress takes its toll on everyone around you, not just you. The daily living demands, such as bills, kids, and jobs, all take their toll on you. Left uncontrolled, this stress will adversely affect your health, your body, your mind, and your immune system.

Stored-up stress can contribute to symptoms and issues related to:

- *Digestive health*
- *Inflammation*
- *Immune system*
- *Bone density*
- *Sexual health*
- *Sleep*
- *Anxiety*
- *Irritability*
- *Increased sugar levels*

Ever wonder why you are feeling so negative for no apparent reason? Here are some of the not-so-obvious side effects of too much stress and lack of focus in your life:

- Snapping at husband/wife/kids/animals/co-workers
- Anger issues
- Being exhausted and having no energy at the end of the day
- Forgetfulness
- Fractured focus
- Build-up of clutter—physical, mental, and electronic

- Eating to compensate for negative feelings
- Weight loss or gain
- Increased drinking
- Increase in medication for anxiety
- Depression
- Sleeplessness
- Not getting enough REM sleep
- Becoming or having become a drug addict or alcoholic
- Forgetting important occasions
- Being late for appointments
- Seldom laughing
- Being unproductive and inefficient at work
- Having no time for others
- Cannot be counted on by others
- Self-invalidation
- Self-mutilation
- Erosion in your confidence level and self-esteem
- Causing car accidents through lack of focus and sleep
- Increase in hospital visits, and eventually hospitalization, possibly resulting in disease, heart attack, stroke, etc.

This negative list goes on and on . . . and you likely have dealt with many of these effects at one point or another in your own life.

However, the same can also be said that by applying these *4 Simple Words*, the list of positive results can be equally long. Before even implementing any other strategies, you can start to enjoy the benefits of an uncluttered lifestyle.

Let's be clear that taking small initial steps is key to creating larger changes in your life. When you are overwhelmed and stressed, it can be difficult to figure out how to end that cycle. It just becomes a constant loop that we have all dealt with. Even when you break out from under this cycle for a moment, without a true strategy to stay out, you will end up in the black hole of clutter and constant work again.

> *"Nature is pleased with simplicity, and nature is no dummy."*
>
> **Isaac Newton,** English mathematician, physicist, astronomer, theologian, author

Some positive results of a simplified, less stress-filled life:

- Kindness and compassion to others
- Patience with husband/wife/kids/animals/co-workers
- Plenty of energy left over at the end of the day

- Better/improved focus
- More personal inner joy
- Open willingness to take the time to help others
- Reduction in clutter
- Moderation when drinking
- No need to be on anxiety or anti-depression medication
- Sleeping well (getting enough REM sleep)
- Remembering and celebrating special occasions
- On time for appointments
- More productive and efficient
- Laughing often
- Making time for others
- Able to be counted on by others
- A healthy confidence level and good self-esteem
- Not causing car accidents
- Little time spent in hospitals, with no major stress induced illness

Now imagine for a second that you were actually enjoying these benefits. How would that impact the overall quality of your life?

This is a "**Motivational Moment**":

Kim loves to volunteer and give back to her community, aside from being a busy entrepreneurial businesswoman, wife, and mother. This is what Kim has to say about using just one step of my "5 Steps to Success" system:

> *"Jeannette became my hero when she introduced me to the Three Basket system. While this concept is so simple, it really helped me to organize the numerous pieces of paper coming into my home office. With multiple lines of business, volunteer, and personal responsibilities, I process a lot of information on a monthly basis. Now, on my admin day, at a quick glance, I can see what needs to be handled this week, what is pending, and what needs to be filed. Even my family knows that if they want me to do something for them, it goes in the INBOX. Simple, easy steps, but they make all the difference when it comes to maintaining an efficient and organized workspace."*
>
> **Kim Gervais**
> Independent Travel Agent

Your Natural Rhythm of Life

Make sure you schedule some regular personal recharging time, daily or weekly. This step is vital to include as part of your personal work policy or business plan.

We are all interrupted so many times in one day that most people walk around with chronic fractured focus. By using The Golden Timer to remind you when to take personal down time, you will be investing in your life, and you will move away from the effects of chronic fractured focus and confusion.

Another piece of the puzzle that can help you is to have a mantra for yourself.

Definition – Mantra: A sound, word, or phrase, or sacred verbal formula, repeated in prayer, meditation, or incantation, which is repeated often, or that expresses someone's basic beliefs. One suggestion (of course) to help you create your new positive habits for success, is to repeat the words, *predictability, simplicity,* and *stress relief*. Just an idea!

Are you ready for a positive mindset shift? If you are, then read on to the next chapter.

Chapter 8

SHAME, BLAME, AND REGRETS

You now know that lack of personal organization takes its toll on your life.

Studies have shown that women are more likely than men to report stress, and they react to a wider range of stressors. Women tend to report higher levels of chronic strains stemming from time constraints, others' expectations, marital relationships, children, and family health. It has even been suggested that women are socially conditioned to be more responsive to others' well-being, so their higher stress rates may partially stem from this nurturing role.

Your negative emotions diminish confidence in yourself and your abilities. When left to fester, they quite literally can stop you where you stand.

Shame or blame, and everyone's favourite, *regret* for things not done or something that you did do, are negative emotions. Being under constant stress compromises your immune system, and this can start to wear out your heart as well as many other internal organs.

It is a fact that when you are stressed, it releases multiple hormones, based on your flight, fight, or freeze response. The truth is that we are not meant to live in a constant state of an adrenaline rush.

The good news is that you are not alone!

Living a life feeling overwhelmed and defeated is a negative, draining, life-sucking emotion, with no redeeming features whatsoever.

Being Mindful in the Right Way

One of the ways to create a reduction in your stress is to first and foremost apply the "mantra" of the *4 Simple Words,* to situations you will run into in your life. The words, as you of course know by now, are: *predictability, simplicity,* and *stress relief.*

An improved mindset is one of stress reduction, which will occur naturally once you have reduced the drama, confusion, and unpredictable nature of how you have been running your life. Your two foundation stones of predictability and simplicity can be your guiding principles for improvement.

To get to a calmer place in your life, you first need to change the way you have been running it so far. You can be whatever you decide to be, but you first need to get into action on a personal level to change the way you have been functioning.

What Makes You Really Happy?

In addition to all of what I have written above, the key to happiness is knowing what recharges you, delights your soul, and helps to keep you motivated. So many people have no idea what makes them feel happy and re-energized.

While on stage, I once asked my audience to put up their hands if they knew what made them happy and brought joy into their lives. Only one quarter of the room put their hands up. Sad.

So, take some time for yourself, and learn what feeds you positively and emotionally. For me, being in the country amongst nature, especially with animals around, will recharge my batteries and elevate my mood into a higher emotional level.

Is spending a day at a downtown spa your favourite thing to do, or do you like to spend time reading a favourite book, undisturbed? Perhaps it is spending time with your kids, or doing a hobby you love. Carve out some time each week to recharge your emotional batteries, doing what makes you feel happy. Life will seem the sweeter for it.

Stop wasting time, and just ask them!

Look around you—why are others succeeding more than you? They have the exact same twenty-four hours that you do, yet they get more accomplished. How are they doing this? What are their secret steps to attaining their goals? Have you ever asked them what their most successful actions are to date? Why not ask them? Do not waste time trying to re-invent the wheel when someone has already successfully done it. In my experience, whenever I have asked someone about their successful actions, they were flattered to be asked. It is affirmation that their success has been noticed and appreciated. So, ask!

You will discover that they had certain preparatory steps that they did, or always do, as part of their next expansion or goal attainment.

Transitioning—Are You Up for It?

> *"The secret of change is to focus all your energy not on fighting the old, but on building the new."*
> **Socrates**, classical Greek philosopher

At this point in your life, if you do not have even the vaguest flicker of hope in your heart that you will succeed in creating positive transitions in your life, then you will not. That mindset is self-fulfilling. In that case, close this book and walk away now.

But if you have even the slimmest idea that you might, just possibly, *maybe*, succeed, then read on, as there is now a world of positive options and opportunities waiting for you to step into.

Self-improvement always starts with a decision or agreement within yourself to transition or change the way you have been functioning up until now. Obviously, things have not been working the way you wanted them to, or you would not be reading this!

> **CALL TO ACTION**
>
> - To further cement your commitment to a better life, I recommend you create an agreement or contract with yourself that you are going to be active in your transition to a new, happier, simpler, less stressful life. This means, of course, that you will actively apply the *4 Simple Words* steps and The Golden Timer to your life, as a guide towards your personal success.
>
> - If you go to www.GettingOutFromUnderBook.com, you will find a personal contract there. Print it out, sign it, and date it. Then put it somewhere you can see it on a daily basis to remind you of your new commitment of personal success you have entered into with yourself.
>
> - It is always best to have an accountability partner. Once your personal contract has been downloaded, signed, and dated, I would love to see it—so feel free to send me a copy of your new contract!
>
> - Wouldn't it be nice to wake up in the morning refreshed and looking forward to what you know you want, and knowing what you can accomplish for that day, week, month, and year?

It is possible, really. Read on . . .

> *"Too many of us are not living our dreams because we are living our fears."*
>
> **Les Brown**, American author and internationally renowned speaker

This is a "**Motivational Moment**":

"Jeannette helped me to organize my condominium apartment in 2014. At that time, I was in the midst of separation and divorce, and my mood and energy was very low. I had no mental energy to keep my space organized and functional, and my apartment was a total mess. I was ashamed to bring anyone to my place, and didn't have proper space to eat, cook, rest or relax. With her great system, and through a simple process that she developed, Jeannette not only helped me to reduce my paper mess and organize my space, but she also showed me how to keep it organized. It had a significant impact on my mental and physical health. Also, as a result of having a more organized, spacious and beautiful space, I was able to bring in a tenant and increase my income. Thank you, Jeannette, for all your help—you are great!"

Dr. Mandana Attarzadeh
Author, 2020 recipient of the "Woman of Worth Award" and "International Women Achievers Award," speaker, and women's empowerment coach,
Toronto, Ontario
fb.me/theflourishingwoman

If you want to know how to gain confidence and improve your health, then the next few pages will be helpful to you.

Chapter 9

BREAKING THROUGH TO YOUR OWN SUCCESS!

In an attempt to get a break from this feeling of being overwhelmed, and from the stress accompanying it, some people turn to overindulgence of food, gambling, or recreational drugs. These negative actions just add to one's stress, which in turn also leads to shortened tempers, destroyed relationships, and sometimes even domestic violence. As well, it is a widely held belief that stress is a precursor of poor health.

A study from Stats Canada (2 Oct 2006, risk factors associated with violence against women) shows that out of various sources of stress, chronic strains such as continuing problems with crowded schedules, finances, and relationships, appeared to be the most potent reasons for this.

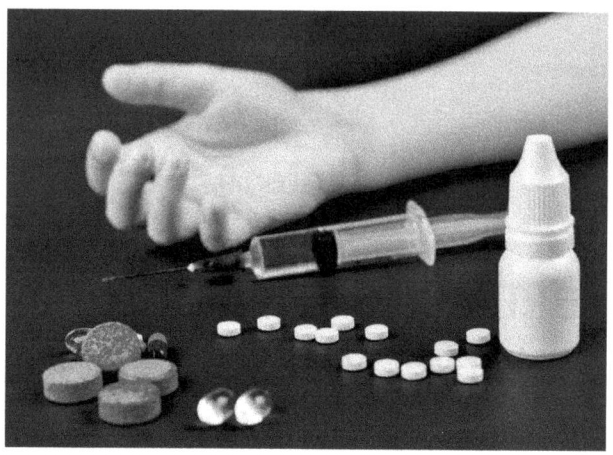

When it comes right down to it, stress is among our greatest health threats. It's been linked to complications like high blood pressure, heart disease, obesity, and diabetes. It can also present immune issues, higher risk of infertility and miscarriage, headaches, muscle tension or pain, anxiety, and depression.

Researchers at Wayne State University in Detroit have even found that a mother's stress levels directly impact the brain development of their baby in-utero; and more specifically that the mother's stress can actually change the neural connectivity of her unborn baby's brain.

Food for thought . . .

> *"The biggest adventure you can ever take is to live the life of your dreams."*
>
> **Oprah Winfrey,** American media executive, talk show host, actress, television producer, and philanthropist

Lack of Confidence

Confidence is born out of accomplishment, and so your first tool in growing your success, is and always will be your ability to prepare for what is coming ahead.

Gaining predictability is the groundwork for your future accomplishments, which is the first mantra step of *4 Simple Words*. When you create more predictability, then you start to regain confidence in your own ability to address the clutter in all areas of your life.

Of course, self-discipline is a key part in maintaining good habits. It is the difference between having a positive or negative mindset for yourself. So, it is up to you to fail or succeed once you know about the power you gain from applying *4 Simple Words* to your life. Use The Golden Timer to help keep you on track.

> *"Nothing in life is to be feared; it is only to be understood. Now is the time to understand more, so that we may fear less."*
> **Marie Curie**, Polish scientist, Nobel Peace Prize in physics and chemistry

How to Find Your Way Out of an Assumed Mental Problem!

The definition of **focus** is "to direct your attention or effort at something specific."

As mentioned previously, when you are overwhelmed, your ability to focus is greatly reduced. Your ability for prolonged concentration is near to impossible. In short, your attention span shrinks.

Some of my clients, when I first meet them, confess that they think they might have developed a mental problem, because they are experiencing some level of memory loss. Central to their concern are anxiety attacks and an inability to focus and to retain recent facts.

I can tell you from observable first-hand experience that for those clients who have actively applied *4 Simple Words* into their lives, they have rapidly regained the ability to focus and remember things again.

One key step to operating in a better organized, more efficient lifestyle, is the ability to quickly locate things—just like finding those darn car keys when you need them!

CALL TO ACTION

- Uncluttering is a layered process, so keep returning to it.
- To continue to assist you to nibble at the problem of physical clutter, write down three things you know right now that you can get rid of in your environment.
- Go into action and reduce, organize, or toss those three physical things cluttering you. Give them to a charity you like, or re-gift them, but get them out of your space.
- Make a self-promise that you will ALWAYS put the things you use regularly, back into their permanent homes—just like those car keys—and your life will suddenly become less complicated and stress-free through that small, simple action.
- Now write down how you felt before you did this exercise.
- Take a moment to check on yourself, and write down how you feel now that you have actually identified one thing that you know you can do to make you happy.

If you feel that you are really ready to tackle a more involved uncluttering process for your life, then there is an online Extension Course that takes a more thorough and in-depth walk through the "Call To Action" steps, and much more!

Go to: www.GettingOutFromUnderBook.com

There are other tools that can be added to increase focus (and improve your sleep), but the best platform to start with that I have seen over the years is the policy or mantra of *4 Simple Words.*

Chapter 10

BRINGING 4 SIMPLE WORDS INTO YOUR PROFESSIONAL LIFE

Now that you have started to apply the *4 Simple Words* and The Golden Timer into your personal life, congratulations! Now, how about introducing your staff to this?

In the business world, personal efficiency is everything

This still applies today. The General Social Survey, conducted in 2010, found that educated, white-collar professionals were more likely to report their job as the largest source of stress, 45 per cent of whom had an annual income of $100,000 or more. Immigrants, visible minority groups, and those without a post-secondary education were more likely to pin their stress on finances.

Just because you can do something quickly does not automatically mean it is the most effective solution, or that it is done to the best of your ability. Costly mistakes can be made from rushing to get something done.

Have you ever calculated the price of overwhelming disorganization and the lack of personal time management in your office or business, and how it effects your bottom line?

In 2018, Salary.com reported, in its annual Wasting Time at Work Survey, that 89 percent of respondents admitted that they waste time at work each day. A small percentage even admitted that they waste at least half of an eight-hour workday on non-work-related tasks.

There were 61 percent who admitted to wasting 30 minutes to an hour at work. For a small business owner, even 30 minutes each day adds up to 2.5 hours a week, and 130 hours each year, is a lot. The top electronic time waster at work, in 2017, was Facebook; and in 2018, Google won the prize. Either way, the cost of lost productivity can be crippling, and will be higher in today's media-addicted society.

Way back in 2009, *The Wall Street Journal* published a study that I believe still holds true to this day. It indicated that the average employee wastes nearly six weeks a year looking for information and "things" in their office that they need. I believe that this will only have increased since that time, especially digitally. To get a rough idea on this, multiply six weeks by the number of your employees and their salaries for that time period. Now that's a real money drain hole of inefficiency!

Just How Important is That Meeting Anyway?

One of the biggest non-productive activities in business is "the meeting." Most do little more than waste time and overburden those in attendance. To illustrate this, I am now going to quote some American statistics found in *The Globe* here, but they can apply to Canada and other countries or companies.

In the US, $37 billion (USD) is spent a year on unnecessary meetings, with 73% of the attendees doing other work during that time. Some 45% of the attendees feel overwhelmed by all those (unnecessary) meetings.

So why is so much time wasted in these meetings? I would offer up that bad time management skills, along with a lack of personal efficiency and organization on the part of the executives, are at the bottom of this. The cause of this estimated $37 billion is actually from both you and your employees not having good personal organizational skills in how to run your personal life and business, without becoming overwhelmed, confused, and unfocused. It ultimately boils down to how each individual functions on a personal level. This is immediately reflected on how well (or not) they function within a business team or run a household.

So, as you can see, there is plenty of food for thought on why it is a good idea that you attain some improved personal efficiency and organizational skills to unclutter and increase focus and clarity, and be successful in your business life.

How do you motivate staff productivity and efficiency in the face of electronic distractions?

Wasting time through electronics while at work has become an epidemic in society today. It feeds procrastination, fractures focus and reduces productivity, and increases overwhelm. In fact, a recent survey of 3,200 people, done by Salary.com, found that 64% of employees visited non-work-related websites while at work, every single day.

That can really eat away at your profits!

There are 30% of your staff who spend one hour or less per week wasting work hours on non-work-related sites such as Facebook and LinkedIn, to name just a few. Then you have 29% spending two hours per week wasting time. There are 5% who waste an average of five hours per week, while

3% are guilty of spending more than 10 hours every single week at work on unrelated job sites. That is a lot of money being paid to employees for no production at all.

Like I said, it can really add up!

Of those employees that are guilty of this time wastage, 73% are within the age range of 18–35 years and admit to "meandering" on their computers on a daily basis. The main justifications they give for slacking off at work, is a lack of corporate incentive, or that they do not feel challenged enough—in actual fact, they are bored.

You may think the less educated, less experienced employees waste the most amount of time, but you would be mistaken.

In reality, it is your most well-educated employees who are your worst offenders, with 67% of them having PhDs, and 66% of those having bachelor's degrees, and 65% having master's degrees.

To stem the tide of this epidemic of inefficient use of work-time, it will be up to the leaders of these organizations to re-evaluate how to keep their employees engaged—or they can just continue to pay their employees to surf the web for fun while at work.

Stress and the Workplace

One in four Canadians cite stress as the reason for leaving their job, while 73 per cent of all working adults, aged 20 to 64, report having some level of stress. With work as the leading cause of stress for most of our population, it is more important than ever to learn what you can do to reduce this situation for yourself and those around you.

The solution is a more planned (predictable) working organization, which will create more efficient and engaged employees, along with a higher team building community. If you are interested in doing this, I am available to help you with a tailor-made workshop. For more information, just go to: GetitngOutFromUnderBook.com.

Where to start with all this overwhelm of electronic clutter?

As mentioned earlier, the accumulation of electronic clutter and stress is fast becoming a major problem for most people. Just like you, some people struggle all their lives with the *Clutter Triangle*. This is a continuous build-up of clutter, both physically, mentally, and electronically, with no understanding of how to get control of it, or what to do to actually get rid of the clutter. So, the collection just keeps building, and the stress builds along with it.

Every single person I know reaches a point of being overwhelmed when it comes to their emails.

To help combat this, I suggest you start by consolidating all your scattered pieces of information into a single area/document/data base.

For your contact information, choose one database and use that exclusively. It could be Gmail, Microsoft Outlook, Mailchimp, or what is called a CRM (Customer Relationship

Management) program. Whatever it is, it needs to be able to store basic contact information, as well as have the ability to separate them into different categories for each contact. You cannot remember all the details about each person—don't even try—so you need a database that will be of service to you in that regard.

Just as I mentioned previously in this book, do a spring clean of your electronic clutter—at worst case, every quarter. Delete all the old emails you have accumulated, or *archive* those that you want or need to keep every quarter. Better yet, immediately delete those unwanted emails as they come in. Unclutter your electronic attention-getting bits of emails, photos, and texts.

> *"It is impossible to live without failing at something, unless you live so cautiously that you might as well not have lived at all—in which case, you fail by default."*
>
> **J. K. Rowling,** British novelist

I used to be organized . . .

Born from my many years of experience as a professional organizer, those people that are naturally organized are in the minority, believe me. However, they too have a breaking point. How often have I heard clients tell me, "I was well organized right up until I had my second, third . . . child?" "I had it together until I got sick/had an accident," or, "My parent got sick for months/years. Now I just don't have the energy to handle the backlog and clutter build-up. It is now just too overwhelming to even look at, let alone deal with."

A simple, basic step to get back on track and in control of your life, apart from *4 Simple Words* and The Golden Timer, is to remember to apply the acronym of POP!

> *"Cultivate order before confusion sets in."*
> **Lao Tzu,** Chinese philosopher

HOW TO WORK SMARTER, NOT HARDER

What simple steps can you apply to make your life easier?

"POP": Plan . . . Organize . . . Put it back . . .

Plan and think AHEAD! Work out how to manage your time better so that you spend less time doing the things you HAVE to do, and have more time to do what you really want to do, and which makes you feel happier.

Organize your STUFF so that things have specific homes—somewhere for them to stay until you need them. Anything you use on a daily basis should be stored closer to you; anything you use once a week or once a month, can live further away from where you sit.

Put it back – When you have finished using something, always put it back where you took it from. (You will save yourself time and stress the next occasion you want to find and use it.)

This is particularly important in an office setting.

ABOUT THE AUTHOR

Jeannette Hay was born in Montreal, Canada, and then at age four, her family moved to England, where she was educated and raised until the age of eighteen, when she moved alone to live and work in Spain until she turned twenty-one.

She then moved briefly back to England before studying graphic design at George Brown College, Toronto, Canada.

After living and travelling extensively in various countries, she returned in 2005 to her native country, where she now lives on the outskirts of Toronto, Ontario, Canada.

The award-winning author is also a past chair of the Toronto Professional Organizers in Canada Association, as well as being a fine artist and a seasoned speaker and workshop host. She is available for presentations as well as private one-on-one coaching sessions as *The Overwhelm Coach*. For more information, please contact: *jeannette@GettingOutFromUnderBook.com*.

If you have been inspired by this book, then the best thing you can do is pass it on to someone you know who needs the help to get out from under a stress-filled life.

To order more *Getting Out From Under* books, go to Amazon.com or to GettingOutFromUnderBook.com.

TESTIMONIALS

As a COACH:

*"My summer goals are 90% complete.
Thanks so much; you taught me how to get unstuck! No more overwhelming feelings of panic.
Enjoy the rest of the summer."*

Pam Tishler

"Praise for Jeannette Hay. Over the last several years, Jeannette has been instrumental in getting my home and office organized and in a very zen place, making the rest of my busy life a much more peaceful place. She's a true treasure."

Bobbi Benson, Financial Manager

A Manager's Rescue:
"When things take off with work, it is a glorious thing but can also be overwhelming. Last thing you want to do is slow it down. That's where Jeannette from "Get Me Organized!" comes in."

Betty Hynes, Communications Dir. Crossroad Mgmt.

"My time with Jeannette was invaluable . . . when you are running a small business, you have little time to organize, so getting Jeannette to help me was the best decision for getting it done! I use all the things she taught me, each and every day, and I have more room in my head for creative thoughts and planning now that Jeannette GOT ME ORGANIZED.

Thanks Jeannette, for everything . . . especially my new color-coded filing—it is soooo beautiful!"

Enza Tiberi-Checchia, Mental Health Advocate; Speaker and Founder, Mietcetera.com; Chief Visionary Officer and Co-Founder, Hatsonforawareness.com

"Working with Jeannette has changed the way I manage my business. Her advice and practical ideas and plans have made the day-to-day management so much easier. She has showed me how to organize my staff, my paperwork, and my management team. Her term, 'predictability creates simplicity,' has truly made a difference in my life. Thank you for allowing me to take a step back and look at the big picture, and for helping me to get out of my own head so that I am better equipped to deal with the challenges of being self-employed. I highly recommend her services."

Karen Marth, CEO and Owner of Core Cleaning, www.corecleaning.ca

"Wow. Thanks so much for bringing to life my most favourite poem, a line of which is now my personal mind movie and mantra. 'I am the captain of my ship, the master of my fate.' You made it so simple with The Golden Timer, which was truly a wakeup call for me, and the 4 Simple Words reduced my stress immensely."

Helen Goodman, Financial Coach, Real Estate Investor

"After hearing you speak at a networking meeting, I had you come into my office and help me organize. As a result, I am able to get through my work more quickly AND keep it organized. Thank you."

Sue Hosang, Entrepreneur

"The Golden Timer is the greatest thing since sliced bread, and like a loaf of bread, you eat it one bite at a time."

Jeannette coached me through two major "get out from under" projects. One to declutter my house, to get ready for a renovation, and the other my office. Jeannette's organizational skills, compassion without pity, and a calm "let's do this" attitude brought both projects to timely conclusions. One of the best of the many techniques she gave me was The Golden (10 minute) Timer. I still use it to this day. How do you "get out from under"? It's amazing what you can get done one 10-minute slice at a Golden Time!"

Janet Wilcox, Author, Past President and Founder of Stardate Projects Inc.

I would highly recommend Jeannette's services to anyone with an organizing project. She will help get the job done, and it will improve your whole outlook on life to have more order in it. I really appreciate her support and care. Thanks Jeannette!

Melanie Dickson-Smith, Owner Upbeat Piano Studio Inc. https://upbeatpianostudio.com

"Jeannette's knowledge and expertise was much appreciated in reorganizing our company structure. Just after a couple of meetings the organizational chart took shape, the way I wanted it. Her 4 Simple Words system and the use of the Golden Timer have really helped to make things less stressful. She is very professional and caring and has ensured that I will not go down the time-wasting rabbit-hole, so I can focus now on reaching my goals!"

Naveed Hyder, Founder & Principal Designer, www.h5interiors.com

As a SPEAKER:

"Jeannette's dedication to her craft comes through loud and clear in her presentation.

I would highly recommend booking Jeannette if you have a group that has interest in creating a more functional and pleasing space in their office or in their home. You will come away with some useful tips to get started on right away. For those needing individual and on-going attention,

I recommend a consultation with Jeannette so that she can address your personal needs."

Marlene Marco, Founder of Heart of Networking, https://www.heartofnetworkingevents.com/

"*Jeannette is a fabulous speaker. She brings a high level of energy and enthusiasm into any meeting. You'll get relevant and valuable information and have a few laughs at the same time. Her talks are very informative and motivational, and I can highly recommend her.*"

Uli Philps, Neat4Ever, http://neat4ever.ca/

"*Jeannette is an inspirational, upbeat woman. She can speak to a crowd with class and style. She is very in tune with the needs and wants of her clients and colleagues. She is a consummate professional and a true credit to her profession.*"

Christine Henderson of Henderson Automotive (Lady owned and operated since 1998)

"*I have had a couple of opportunities to hear Jeannette speak. Her ability to reach everyone in the audience always excites me. Her topics are always current and relative, and I always walk away with many nuggets of useful and usable information. She has a unique way of reaching people, and she truly understands what the business owner goes through. If Jeannette is speaking, I cannot miss the event!*"

Karen Marth, Owner of Core Cleaning, http://corecleaning.ca/

"Presenter Jeannette Hay, of Get Me Organized!, did a presentation on the importance of time management and organization to students from Grades 6, 7, and 8, at St. Albert Elementary School, in Scarborough, ON. For 90 minutes, she gave her entertaining and educational presentation to over 100 people. We feel very fortunate to have had Jeannette speak to us. She was very friendly and answered all of our questions expertly. The students all now understand how improved organization and time management can help them in their schoolwork and moving forward, both in their personal and future professional lives. I strongly recommend Jeannette's presentation to any school that would like to improve their students' work ability, and gain time management skills."

John Sawdon, Grade 7 Teacher

"Jeannette is a captivating speaker. She engages the audience with relevant info and examples. Her presentations are organized, well thought through, and easy to listen to."

HM, Entrepreneur

"Jeannette engages so easily with her audience. She is sincere, passionate, and always has something of benefit to share."

CJ, Business owner, Toronto

"Jeannette provides a warm and welcoming environment to her participants, and is always knowledgeable, prepared, calm, and inclusive when she facilitates."

DK

"I have heard Jeannette speak and I highly recommend that you hear her too.
She is warm, funny and very informative.
Check her out for yourself."

Charlene Day, Author and co-author of 11 books (6 international bestsellers), Treasure Coach
http://healthandwealthglobal.com

NOTE FROM THE AUTHOR

> *"Nothing will work unless you do."*
>
> **Maya Angelou**, American author, poet, singer, and civil rights activist

Now that you have read through this book, I hope you are feeling more confident and empowered, knowing that you now have the tools you can use in any situation where you start to feel overwhelmed. Remember that reading the information is not nearly as important as actually applying what you have learned.

It all boils down to your willingness to get into action in applying these steps. I wish you all the best in getting out from under and breaking free from stress and overwhelm! Get ready for a happier, healthier, and a more successful life in a world crafted by you, moving towards the life you have always wanted.

I cannot wait to hear from you on any successes you have experienced in applying the tools from this book; I would be honoured to share these wonderful moments with you.

There are a lot more tools and tips I can give you to increase your abilities, both in your personal and professional lives.

To get access to the next level of your abilities, you can attend one of my online webinars, in-person workshops, or invest in yourself by having me as your coach.

Additionally, if you have any questions or would like to have me as your personal and confidential cheerleader and guide in coaching you, or wish for me to speak at your event or to your staff, or have me as a guest on your show, please go to my website, or email me at:

jeannette@GettingOutFromUnderBook.com

For the Extension Course, bonuses, illustrations, and the downloadable Personal Contract, and one-on-one coaching, go to: **GettingOutFromUnderBook.com**.

To your success!

Jeannette
Award-Winning Author

www.ingramcontent.com/pod-product-compliance
Lightning Source LLC
Chambersburg PA
CBHW061604110426
42742CB00039B/2812